COMMODITIES: 50 THINGS YOU REALLY NEED

Peter Sainsbury

For my sons, Rohan and Mika.

Contents

Acknowledgements

Thank you to friends, family and colleagues for your great feedback. Thank you Dr Angela Stokes (AcEDemy) for editing my book and pulling it into shape. Last, but not least thanks to my wife, Anita for your support and giving me the space to write this book.

Introduction

Commodities are the building blocks of life. We rely on commodities to support our daily existence. From steel and copper to build our homes, gas and coal to heat them, gasoline to fuel our cars so we can travel to work and wheat and corn for food.

Most books about commodities sell you the dream that you can give up your day job and make a killing by trading soybeans. Some suggest that you should invest your pension in gold and a basket of other commodities and look forward to a prosperous retirement. The others are full of complex statistics that are impenetrable to most people. Judgments

This book is different. It aims to show you why paying attention to commodities will help you understand everything from the cost of living to geopolitical developments going on around the world and the implications for your investments. This book will give you the 50 things you *really* need to know.

Whether you are involved in producing commodities, buy them for your business, want to trade or invest in them or simply – like the rest of us – consume them on a daily basis, this book should have something for you. In a book that starts with "50 Things…" there is a limit to how much detail I can give, but where possible I have identified sources for further reading.

I hope that after reading this book you will see the world anew. Instead of just eating your breakfast you will be wondering what impact the latest geopolitical crisis will have on the supply of wheat for your cereal, or what impact Chinese demand will have on the price of milk. Later, on the way to work, you might hear about a hurricane in the United States (US) Gulf and suddenly think I had better fill my car up before it affects the price of oil.

Understanding commodity markets and their implications will become increasingly important over the next 50-100 years as the global population expands, environmental risks become more acute and the risk of supply disruption for businesses grows.

At the same time, the above factors – as well as many more outlined in this book – represent an opportunity. Understanding how changes in the price of a commodity affect your investments may help you make better judgments about where to place your retirement capital, as well as providing an opportunity for businesses and innovators to offer something that overcomes the latest commodity bottleneck.

This book does not have to be read as a continuous narrative. Each of the 50 things should make sense on their own, although I have highlighted where you might benefit from looking at another chapter. At the end of each chapter, I have provided a summary of "the essential thing" to take away.

On writing this book I would like to thank the coal and gas that generated the electricity that powered my laptop and lit my office late into the evening, the lithium battery in my smartphone that helped with my research and the coffee that kept me going...

If after reading this book you found it entertaining and you learnt something new then please consider leaving a review wherever you bought this e-book. They really do make a difference.

About the author

Peter Sainsbury is the founder of Materials Risk. Disillusioned by the mainstream press' sole focus on commodity trading and investment, Peter decided to start Materials Risk to help actual commodity buyers, as well as investors, sift through the noise and discover issues important to them, in an age in which commodity prices no longer just go up.

Disclaimer

All views expressed in "**Commodities: 50 Things You Really Need to Know**" are those of the author alone and not the view of any associated company or employer. This book will not be offering any investment advice, so please don't sue me if you think I am.

Peter Sainsbury, 2015
materials-risk.com

1) The basics of supply and demand

"From the taste of wheat it is not possible to tell who produced it, a Russian serf, a French peasant or an English capitalist."

Karl Marx

At its basic level a commodity is an input into the production of a good or service – the lithium used in the battery powering the device you're reading this book on, for example. In general, households rarely purchase commodities directly; rather they are typically the raw materials purchased by manufacturing companies to be refined into the goods and services that we use.

One of the basic characteristics of a commodity is that it should be uniform in quality and lacking in product differentiation. Fungibility, as it is known, means that the market treats its instances as equivalent, or nearly so, with no regard to who produced them. Given these properties, one of the characteristics of a commodity is that its price is determined as a function of its market as a whole. In reality, things are not quite so simple and so there is a spectrum of commodification. Few commodities have complete differentiability and hence fungibility. Even wheat is not a uniform commodity. Bread makers prefer "hard" varieties with more protein, and cracker makers prefer "soft" wheat.[1]

The three main categories of commodities are: energy, metals and agriculture. However, the term "commodity" can also be extended to other things, many of which you would not even consider, but share the same properties: internet bandwidth, water or carbon emission credits, for example.

The demand for a particular commodity is closely connected to the demand for a related product or service - known as "derived demand". For example, the demand for steel and many other metals is strongly linked to the demand for new vehicles and other manufactured products, so when an economy goes into a recession, we expect the demand for those metals to also decline or at least not grow as fast.

In order to understand the level of demand you need to know something about the price elasticity of demand (the responsiveness of consumption to a change in the price). As prices rise, will consumption start to wane or will it stay constant (called perfect elasticity of demand)? Typically, if a good is seen as a necessity the price elasticity will be low (otherwise known as inelastic), meaning that an increase in its price will only lead to a relatively small drop in demand. Remember though, what is considered a necessity in the US and other developed economies (gasoline, for example) may be considered a luxury in other parts of the world.

The availability of substitutes also affects a particular commodity's price elasticity of demand. If there are many alternatives (eg, you and I may decide to eat more pasta made from Durum wheat if the price of rice increases) then a commodity is likely to be price elastic.

Increasingly, commodities are being seen as financial assets and so are in demand for their own sake. In contrast to other assets though (eg, a stock, bond or property), a commodity provides no income stream. Some commodities like gold and many other precious metals are seen as a store of value in times of uncertainty.

The supply of commodities responds to incentives. High demand and high prices typically encourages farmers, miners and other commodity producers to respond by increasing supply in order to capture higher margins. However, supply is also sticky. In economic terms, commodity supply tends to be price inelastic, ie, it takes time for supply to respond, whether it is a mine, planting crops and waiting for the harvest or drilling an oil well. The supply of commodities is also prone to disruption and can be affected by many factors: adverse weather, disease, war, transport problems, environmental damage and cartel behaviour, for example.

As we will see later, changes in commodity prices can affect entire economies, be the spark that causes war and cause damage to the environment and in turn be influenced by the changing climate. In addition, they are often transported across the world to satisfy demand and they are frequently a source of fear and concern for the future.

A bushel of wheat or a tonne of lead look much the same now as they did thousands of years ago. What's changed is what they can be used for, the wide ranging impact they can have and the threat and opportunity that bottlenecks in their supply and demand represent.

The essential thing:

A commodity is an input into the production of a good or service and by definition is uniform in quality, lacks product differentiation and is fungible.

2) Income and population

"No tree grows to heaven."

Wall St adage

Rapid economic growth in China and many other emerging economies was one of the main factors driving commodity prices higher in the early 21st century. As economies grow, industrialise and urbanise, they typically consume increasing amounts of commodities – particularly industrial metals like steel, as well as energy. In particular, there has been rapid economic development in many emerging economies since 2000. Investment in transport networks, electricity grids and housing has increased the demand for industrial commodities and energy.

Economies' demand for commodities typically tends to follow an S-curve. This is where consumption rises at an increasing rate before eventually stabilising at much higher levels. This is when income elasticity of demand comes into play. As economies develop, high income elasticity of commodity demand means that the quantity of commodities demanded rises substantially in response to an increase in income per capita (also known as per person). However, as economies develop the income elasticity gradually declines resulting in smaller increases in commodity demand for a corresponding rise in income.

While there is a broad consensus on the role of income growth in industrial and energy commodities, this is not so for agriculture. Food commodities are subject to Engel's law of less than unitary income elasticity. Engel observed that as income rises, the proportion of income spent on food falls, even if the actual expenditure on food rises. Indeed, the share in global consumption of most agricultural commodities by large emerging economies has not increased as dramatically as often assumed during the recent price boom.

China and India's combined average annual growth in grain consumption was lower in 2002-08 than in 1995-2001. Meanwhile, China has been a net exporter of cereals since the late 1990s, with one exception during 2004-05. Similarly, India has been a net importer of these commodities only once since the beginning of the 21st century, during 2006-07.[2]

Historical patterns show that as countries get richer, their diets change and demand is strongest for finer foods that are higher in proteins, such as meat, dairy, sugar and edible oils. The demand for basic foods, like cereals, peaks at early levels of development, typically when GDP per capita is under $5,000. However, the demand for finer foods climbs as countries shift from low to middle income levels and rises further as people aspire to the good life. This is generally so as GDP per capita levels pass $20,000 and, for some fine foods such as edible oils, demand climbs at an even higher rate as processed foods become more popular.

Greed is also an important factor in affecting the amount and type of food commodities consumed. The Food and Agriculture

Organization of the United Nations (FAO) believes that the typical person needs 1,800 kilocalories (kcals) a day. Yet the world's heavyweights consume approximately twice that figure at 3,600-3,900 kcals per day. But developing nations are catching up too. China and Brazil consume 3,200 and 3,000 kcals a day, respectively – an increase of more than 800 kcals a day in fifteen years. Even countries once blighted by famine are now well over the threshold: Ethiopia now averages 2,000 kcals a head each day versus 1,500 kcals in 1990.[3]

The composition of the commodities that economies consume may also change as economies develop and incomes rise. For example, titanium dioxide is one commodity that could benefit from a consumption driven economy. Its primary use is in the creation of the white pigment used in paints. It remains to be seen if the Chinese and other rapidly growing economies will develop the same appetite for DIY and home improvements, but given their enthusiastic adoption of many other western way of life choices one could expect to see some convergence here as well.

Higher population levels are not the only influence on commodity demand, the composition of the population also has an effect. As the population ages, resulting in a higher ratio of older to younger people, a lower demand for commodities related to construction may result. At the extreme, young adults' demand for construction peaks when they often buy a bigger home to start a family. Equally, employers have to build offices and factories where these young adults can work. But older people already have somewhere to live and are leaving the workplace to retire. Taken together, this influences everything from the demand for timber to polyvinylchloride (more commonly known as PVC and is used to make pipes).

The essential thing:

As economies grow and incomes rise, they tend to require more and more commodities to support that growth; changes in population and income can also affect the composition of the commodities demanded.

3) Stocks

"Stocks are like insurance. You keep them for the bad times."

José Cuesta, World Bank

Gasoline stocks in the New York region were at record lows going into the autumn of 2012, following a series of refinery closures. Little did refiners, logistics companies or, indeed, consumers realise that the weather was about to seriously disrupt their ability to fill up their cars with gasoline. Hurricane Sandy hit New York in late October, causing damage to oil infrastructure, forcing the idling of approximately 70% of refineries on the East Coast, flooding terminals and preventing deliveries of gasoline by ship. At the height of the storm, approximately two-thirds of petrol stations had no gasoline for sale. Gasoline prices saw a brief, albeit small, spike. New York got off lightly on this occasion because of it traditionally being a low demand time of year and the storm delaying consumer's purchases of fuel. What it did highlight, however, was how low stocks had resulted in the region becoming vulnerable to its fuel supplies being disrupted.

Stocks (otherwise known as inventories) act as form of buffer for both producers and consumers of a commodity. Typically, falling stock levels occur if demand increases faster than supply, resulting in a higher commodity price. Falling stock levels may, however, make a particular commodity market more vulnerable to an unanticipated disruption to supply or a sudden increase in demand. Holding stocks has a cost though, known as the cost of carry. This includes storage fees, insurance and the interest rate that could have been earned on the value of the commodities. Some commodities are more suited to storage than others: gold won't degrade but you need more than a padlock to keep it safe, meanwhile agricultural products need to be stored in perfect conditions to preserve them in good condition.

It is important to emphasise that physical commodity markets must clear. Production and storage constraints limit the ability of the market to respond to rapid shifts in demand and so require substantial swings in prices to keep the physical market in balance (see Chapter 22 on commodity volatility). In other words, you can't consume what you don't have and you can't produce what you can't consume or store.

Instead of concentrating on actual stock levels and comparing them with where they are relative to the same time last year, one favoured alternative is to look at the stocks-to-use ratio. This ratio indicates the level of carryover stock for any given commodity as a percentage of the total demand or use.

Data on production, consumption and inventories for most major commodities are often published by commodity exchanges or official agencies at regular intervals. This type of data helps to increase the level of transparency in commodity markets for which it would be difficult and costly for individual participants in the market to carry out themselves. It is eagerly anticipated by consumers, producers and traders, with the latter often taking a view on the data in advance of it being published.

Despite efforts to improve transparency within commodity markets, a significant amount of data remains hidden. Even in major commodity markets like aluminium, stock levels held by companies may be unknown or dependent on estimates.

Perhaps the biggest uncertainty is what proportion of commodities in storage actually represents claims to real physical demand. As we see in Chapter 44, the financialisation of commodities means that investors may now also seek to store a commodity for reasons other than its use, as a means for future consumption and, specifically, using commodities as collateral. As more commodities go into private inventory systems, transparency declines increasing the risk of a price shock in the event of an unexpected jolt to either demand or supply.

The essential thing:

Stocks of commodities act as a form of buffer against unexpected shocks to either demand or supply.

*Want to know more? Visit my blog **Materials Risk** and get email updates and analysis on what's really happening in commodities and commodity markets.*

4) Costs

"…with the relatively rapid exit of supply as prices fell, the veracity of the cost curve data has been tested and validated."

Macquarie Bank

In the long term, the cost of producing a commodity plays a defining role in determining commodity prices. In terms of commodity economics, the cost of production theory of value states that the price of a commodity is determined by the sum of the cost of the resources that went into making it. Commodity production costs include: raw materials, wages, research and development, insurance, licensing fees, taxes and every other cost incurred by real world commodity businesses.

The production cost is measured not only in unit value terms, but also in human lives and the environmental impact. Any physical business managing the inherent risks in exploring for, finding and capturing natural resources from the most hazardous environments must invest heavily in safety and insurance protocols. Moreover, in going to the furthest reaches of the planet to get commodities, producers are increasingly creating the associated social infrastructure: eg, roads, housing, schools, hospitals and grocery stores.[4]

Imagine putting all of these costs together to produce a chart with the producers of a commodity laid out from left to right with the width of each bar indicating the output from each producer (the wider the bar the more they churn out) and the height of each bar showing their average cost per unit production (the higher the more expensive). This results in a commodity cost curve with the low cost producers on the left and the highest cost producers on the right.

You can then overlay the current price of a commodity and then judge which producers (or individual projects) are economic or not. A producer wants to sit in the lowest quartile on the cost curve, increasing the return on their output while also allowing a margin in the event that prices fall. Marginal producers are considered to be those on the right hand side of the chart, beyond the 90th percentile.

Estimating production costs is not without uncertainty and even more so for these marginal producers. For example, a small mine might be found in some far flung part of the world for which there is little or no data. Even if a particular mine is operating at a loss, there is a good chance it will continue to operate. This is because it costs a significant amount of money to close and eventually re-open a mine – so producers will tend to keep operating it for much longer than they would ideally want to. Once the initial investment has been made the incentive remains to continue producing as long as the price remains above the project's operating cost. This will usually be much lower than the breakeven rate or marginal cost of production.[5]

The structural component of price is usually determined by the long-term supply curve or the cost of bringing the last needed unit of the commodity to the market – referred to as the marginal cost of production. Importantly, the impact on price of a change in other market fundamentals (demand, supply and inventories) is not linear. Calling upon incremental fractions of marginal supply becomes increasingly costly, potentially resulting in a higher commodity price.

As supply is generally slower to adjust than demand, given the capital and time intensive nature of commodity production investments, these structural supply side factors typically drive commodity markets on a 2-10 year horizon. Conversely, the cyclical component of price is largely determined by fluctuations in short-term fundamentals, as captured by inventory levels. As demand adjusts over short time horizons, demand is the most important driver of the cyclical component of price and typically dominates the market on a 1-2 year horizon.[6]

Rising marginal production costs, in turn, raise production costs for other commodities – energy, for example, is a vital component of a farm's operating costs. Direct energy consumption includes the use of diesel, electricity, propane, natural gas and renewable fuels for activities on the farm. Indirect energy consumption includes the use of fuel and feedstock (especially natural gas) in the manufacturing of agricultural chemicals, such as fertilisers and pesticides.

Energy makes up a significant part of operating costs for most crops. This is especially true when considering indirect energy expenditure on fertiliser because the production of fertiliser is extremely energy intensive, requiring large amounts of natural gas. For some crops – like oats, corn, wheat and barley – the combined cost of energy and fertiliser make up more than half of the total operating expenses in the US.[7] The proportion of direct to indirect energy use varies by crop though. Corn, for example, is an energy input for ethanol production; it has relatively low direct fuel costs but has the highest percentage of fertiliser costs.

Even though the geology in an area may be ideal for growing or extracting a commodity, political issues manifesting themselves in the form of protectionism and resource nationalism may mean that instead of capital being directed to the most efficient commodity investment it has to go to high cost, inefficient sources, further increasing the marginal cost of production. Indeed even the uncertainty that resource nationalism brings will result in a higher "hurdle rate" (the internal rate of return at which a project would probably go ahead) for commodity production to take place than would otherwise be so (see Chapter 27 for more on resource nationalism). Given that the shifting sands involved in the cost of producing a commodity (geology, other commodity prices, balance sheets, geopolitics, resource nationalism and not to mention the main development costs) are in a constant state of flux, so the marginal cost of production is too. It is a moving target.

The essential thing:

In the long term, the cost of production plays
a defining role in determining commodity
prices.

5) Interest rates

"Let them remain in the ground for our children and grandchildren who need them."

King Abdullah of Saudi Arabia

One factor that is often overlooked when it comes to commodity prices is the impact of monetary policy. Changes in global monetary policy (ie, interest rates and quantitative easing) can have a significant impact on commodity prices and are an important fundamental factor that should be considered alongside demand, supply, stock levels and costs. There is something intuitive about the idea that when the US Federal Reserve "prints money", the money flows into commodities, among other assets, and so increases their prices. But, how exactly does it work?[8]

First, looser monetary policy reduces the cost of storing commodities and thereby increases the demand to hold them. Lower interest rates may also decrease the volatility of commodity prices in response to unexpected shocks. By reducing inventory holding costs, lower interest rates encourage the use of inventories to smooth prices over transient shocks to commodity supply and demand (see more in Chapter 3).

Second, lower interest rates may also incentivise you and other investors to put money into riskier assets like commodities, rather than bonds or equities. Looser monetary policy could also mean that investors' cash is channeled towards riskier investments in emerging economies that will then indirectly result in an increase in demand for commodities.

Third, lower interest rates may also discourage commodity extraction by reducing the value of monetising undeveloped commodity resources on the part of producers, providing a further upward impetus to prices. Hotelling's rule states that the most socially and economically profitable extraction path for a non-renewable resource is one along which the price of the commodity, determined by the marginal net revenue from its sale, increases at the rate of interest.[9]

If the producer of a non-renewable commodity (eg, Saudi Arabia, for oil) believed that crude future prices were not going to keep up with higher interest rates, then they would be better off selling as much as possible for cash and then purchasing bonds. Conversely, if they expected crude prices would increase faster than the prevailing interest rate, they would be better off keeping the oil in the ground (see the quote at the start of this chapter from King Abdullah of Saudi Arabia, when in 2008 he was asked if the country planned to tap newly discovered oil reserves).

It's important to note that, based on Hotelling's rule oil prices would still be determined by supply and demand in the short term, but in the long term output will rise at a rate that means the oil price will only increase at the rate of interest.

Fourth and finally, since most globally traded commodities are priced in US dollars (there are exceptions, rubber, for example, is traded in Japanese Yen), changes in US monetary policy are transmitted through to its currency, either appreciating with tighter monetary policy or depreciating if it is loosened, and in doing so demand for commodities is affected. At its most basic a decrease in the value of the US dollar, relative to a commodity buyer's currency, means that the purchaser will need to spend less of their own currency to buy a given amount of the commodity. As the commodity becomes less expensive demand for the commodity rises, resulting in an increase in the price.

Although a weaker dollar can boost demand, it can also act as a disincentive to producers to increase output. For example, a depreciation of the US dollar against the Chilean peso can reduce profit margins for a copper miner in Chile. All of the miner's revenues will be received in US dollars, which will now buy less pesos, but some proportion of the costs will be denominated in pesos and will remain constant (at least in the short term). Therefore, the prospect of a lower profit margin acts as an incentive to decrease the supply of copper.

Not all commodities will be affected by movements in the dollar in the same way. Those commodities where the market is domestic to the US, with little scope for transportation outside of North America (for example, natural gas and cattle), are likely to see relatively little impact from currency movements.

Commodities tend to be traded in US dollars for two reasons. First, the US dollar is the most freely convertible and liquid currency, with the lowest transaction costs. Second, trading commodities in a single currency makes it easier to compare prices globally, enabling more efficient arbitrage, which should mean lower prices for consumers. The commodity industry chooses to use the US dollar because it makes sense for everyone to do so.

The essential thing:

Monetary policy is one of the main but often forgotten factors affecting commodity prices.

6) Weather

"The longer it goes on without rain the bigger impact it obviously has and this is a big milking time for us so for the dairy sector and some of the numbers I saw were around a billion dollars."

New Zealand Prime Minister John Key

Too much sun, too dry, too wet, too hot or too cold; unless the weather is just right crop yields will undoubtedly suffer. The weather has a significant impact on crop yields and thus overall agricultural production. The wrong type of weather at the wrong time in the planting cycle, even if not prolonged or extreme, can also adversely affect the production of certain crops.

As you see in Chapter 15, an increase in the price of feed grain (perhaps caused by drought) may reduce margins on livestock for farmers. Drought will also reduce the availability and quality of pastureland available. But, by extension, the weather can also affect the supply of livestock and the products derived from them.

Food items with a shorter shelf life and fast production times are particularly vulnerable to extreme weather. High temperatures lead to stressed out cattle and poultry, resulting in less milk and fewer eggs.

Drought can even affect the production of metals. For example, drought in Indonesia can impact nickel production: first, by reducing the hydroelectric electricity generation used to power the mines; and second, by lowering the water levels of the inland waterways that are vital for nickel ore transportation.

The important weather patterns that farmer's all over the world watch out for is the appearance of El Niño or La Niña. These regular, but volatile, weather patterns can cause prolonged changes in weather conditions in significant agricultural producing regions. In terms of commodity producing regions, El Niño typically results in drier conditions across Australia, South East Asia, Brazil and West Africa, but wetter conditions around the southern US states and the coastal areas of South America. La Niña, meanwhile, tends to drench Australia, South East Asia and South America.

If the weather is too windy (a hurricane, for example), then oil rigs and transport facilities operating in the US Gulf are likely to need to shut down or may even suffer damage. If there is a loss of oil production, this may lead to higher oil prices because the region's refineries, which depend on the Gulf's output, are forced to seek crude oil elsewhere.[10]

The US Gulf is also home to significant gas production. During the 2005 season, hurricanes Katrina and Rita knocked out 113 drilling platforms and damaged more than 450 pipelines. As a result, US Gulf natural gas production fell over 10%, causing natural gas prices to spike from $6 per million British thermal units (mBtu) to $14.33 per mBtu.

The demand for energy commodities is also affected by weather. Very warm and very cold temperatures, especially for prolonged periods, can dramatically increase the demand for energy for cooling and heating, respectively, as opposed to the softening effect of more moderate temperatures. Extreme conditions may stress electric transmission and distribution systems or curtail the output of significant energy commodities, resulting in increased maintenance costs and limiting the ability to meet peak customer demand.

The weather always has some form of impact on commodity prices, but the significance is magnified when global stocks are low. Low stock levels may make a particular commodity market more vulnerable to an unanticipated disruption to supply or a sudden increase in demand, whether it is caused by changes in the weather or something else (see Chapter 3).

The weather can sometimes have surprising impacts on seemingly unrelated commodities. In India, for example, the monsoon rains are crucial for the irrigation of crops. So how does the amount of rain falling in India affect the price of gold? Well, India is one of the top consumers of gold and significant amounts of its gold purchases occur in rural regions, with demand heavily dependent on agricultural income. Traditionally, Indian farmers ramp up their gold purchases after a good monsoon and harvest season, using the yellow metal as a store of wealth. With income from farming hit in the event of a bad monsoon season, the funds may not be there to support gold demand.[11]

Producers of commodities understandably concentrate a significant amount of their attention on the weather. However, production decisions often have to be taken months, if not years, in advance, and so there is often very little they can do to react to changes in the weather. Until recently, insurance has been the main tool used by companies to protect against unexpected weather conditions – particularly in more developed countries. However, insurance only provides protection against catastrophic damage, covering high risk and low probability events. Insurance does nothing to protect against the reduced demand that businesses experience because of normal weather variations.

Increasingly, companies have been managing the impact that the weather has on their business through the use of various financial products, commonly referred to as derivatives. While energy companies are still the biggest users of weather risk-related products, farmers are increasingly making use of them too (see Chapter 31 for more discussion on how you can protect yourself from higher and more volatile commodity prices). Note that farmers in poorer countries are much less likely to have the benefit of a safety net, and will therefore face the full force of volatile commodity prices.

Farmers, in particular, are concerned that volatile and extreme climatic variations will only intensify in the future, due to climate change. This will make it more difficult to plan and, perhaps, leading to more volatile agricultural commodity prices (see Chapter 38 for more).

The essential thing:

The weather is a crucial factor that can affect both the supply and the demand for commodities, sometimes in quite unexpected ways.

*Want to know more? Visit my blog **Materials Risk** and get email updates and analysis on what's really happening in commodities and commodity markets.*

7) Commodity cycles

"The cure for high prices is, high prices."

Economic proverb

"An era can be said to end when its basic illusions are exhausted."

Arthur Millar

If you only ever see commodity prices go up, as it was for most of the early part of the 21st century, it can start to feel like a kind of commodity.com, a feeling that prices only ever go in one direction. History doesn't repeat itself, but if often rhymes.[12]

The industrialisation of the US in the late 19th century, and the German build-up prior to World War I, drove an upswing in commodity prices in the early 20th century. The next upswing came after World War II because of the rebuilding of Europe. More recently the industrialisation of Japan, and many other emerging Asian economies, also contributed to an upswing in commodity prices in the 1970s and the early 1980s.

The most recent upswing in commodity prices had its origins in 1998, when prices approached their lowest for 20 years (equal to depression levels, when adjusted for inflation).[13] This was followed by the emergence of China as an industrial force, which drove commodity prices up in the first decade of the 21st century.

Research examining centuries of commodity price data has tended to sketch a pattern of 15-20 year super-cycles (a period of rising prices), followed by a slide in prices over the following 10-15 years when excess investment leads to a flood of supply. The concept of a commodity super-cycle was developed by two economists, among others, working separately: Nikolai Kondratiev in Russia and Joseph Schumpeter in the US.[14]

Kondratiev outlined long waves or cycles spanning 40-60 years. His commodity super-cycle was based on the idea that economic activity gradually rises, and is coupled with low interest rates and rising prices. However, a turning point is reached where asset price bubbles start to form, interest rates rise and economic growth slows. The final phase of the cycle involves recession or depression, and an unwinding of the excesses of the earlier economic boom.

Schumpeter, meanwhile, described periods of short-term volatility that can change the otherwise overriding trend in commodity prices. This change may be driven by an exogenous or unpredictable factor, such as rebuilding a country following a war. Short-term volatility can last a long time, however – for example, 10-15 years if you concentrate on the most recent upswing in commodity prices!

Note that even within these long periods of rising or falling prices there may still be lengthy periods when commodity prices run counter to the longer-term trend. In addition, not all commodities will necessarily behave in the same way during the period of a commodity cycle.

But how does the commodity super-cycle work in practice? Well, both demand and supply for commodities are inelastic in the short term. Essentially this means that it can take quite a long time for consumers and producers to react to pricing signals. When oil prices spike, for example, motorists may have no choice but to continue to use their car to get to work, but eventually they may be able to invest in a more efficient car. Meanwhile, commodity producers take time to invest and then bring on new supplies, ie, exploring for oil and then eventually bringing the crude to market.

In the event that commodity prices rise, there is a significant delay until production begins to respond. Critically, commodity prices do not incentivise new production when investing in a mine or an offshore oil field. Rather, the commodity prices are assumed from feasibility studies and debt and equity raisings. These long-run commodity price assumptions tend to lag behind current commodity prices.

Given that the typical time horizon of a major mine can be as long as 20-30 years, with high initial capital outlay and traditionally slow capital return, the planning process is very risk averse. However, once the economic status warrants a mine being brought into production then it typically takes approximately 7-10 years to take the discovery of a new deposit through to production (although lead times can vary greatly between metals). However, economic and commodity price conditions may be very different when the mine is eventually brought into production. In the event of low commodity prices, producers may find it very difficult to stop production quickly.[15]

Agriculture supply typically responds much faster to changes in underlying demand. The agricultural supply cycle describes the process of activities relating to the growth and harvest of the crop. These include loosening the soil, seeding, watering and harvesting, etc. This cycle can vary from as little as a year for grains such as corn, wheat and soy, to 3-4 years for cocoa, but perhaps even decades such as for forests.

Commodity production generally involves a high ratio of fixed to variable costs that could result in heavy cost penalties in the event that output is suspended. This exacerbates situations of oversupply because the penalties of shutting down production, even when producers are making a loss, may outweigh the decreasing returns from low prices.

Rapid cost appreciation has been a fundamental driver of commodity price levels and commodity price volatility since the commodity price trough in the late 1990s. The powerful economic take off in emerging market demand has called upon costlier and increasingly more difficult to exploit sources of marginal commodity supply. As commodity producers explore further offshore for oil or extract nickel from deeper mines, more and more resources are needed to produce them. The result, when seeing a snapshot of commodity prices in isolation, is that people understandably conclude that prices can only ever go in one direction. Similarly, the sense of euphoria (for investors) or distress (for consumers) at the top of the market is plain to see. Miners, oil prospectors or farmers appear on the front page of Fortune magazine, and otherwise rational people call for commodity prices to permanently reach stratospheric prices.

The signs are there at the bottom of the market too. For example, in 1999 the cover of The Economist declared that we were "Drowning in Oil", and the main article pondered whether the oil price would fall to $5 per barrel. Shortly after that, oil embarked on an eight year long rise to $145 per barrel. Bull markets in commodities tend to end where they start, however. Indeed, evidence suggests that their expected long-run real return (ie, after inflation) is zero.[16]

The price of a commodity acts as an incentive to both consumers and producers. More worryingly though is that governments are not prone to responding to the same price incentives. Instead, the results from a policy point of view can be perverse, perhaps even prolonging the impact of high prices on consumers. For example, governments may, in the belief that prices will continue to rise indefinitely, lock consumers into paying high energy prices to finance investment in generation capacity.

The essential thing:

Commodity prices may rise or fall for a long time.

8) The role of expectations

"...A scarcity or abundance of crops affects the exchange of the world, and tends to forecast future prices, and to give some clue to future production..."

Samuel Benner

"In the business world, the rear view mirror is always clearer than the windshield."

Warren Buffet

The role of expectations is vital in understanding how demand and supply react to a change in the price of a commodity. This point was first illustrated through the Cobweb Theorem, developed in the 1930s. The theory shows how supply and demand responds in a market where the amount produced must be chosen before the price is observed. Agriculture is a great example of where the theory might apply, since there is an interval between planting and harvesting. For example, because of unexpectedly bad weather, farmers go to market with an unusually small crop of wheat, resulting in higher prices. If the farmers expect these high price conditions to continue, then they will plant more wheat relative to other crops in the following year. When the farmers then go to market with the second year's harvested crop, supply will be high, resulting in a drop in the price of wheat. And so it goes on. If farmers then expect low prices to continue, they will reduce the planting of wheat for the subsequent year, resulting in a return to high wheat prices yet again.[17]

Very short-sighted of those farmers, you might say.

Critics of the Cobweb Theorem have argued that rational farmers should be able to work out what the equilibrium level of supply should be, given current information about supply and demand. It is argued that farmers should base their price expectations on how they expect the market is likely to work, rather than just reacting blindly to price movements.[18] However, expectations are not informed predictions of future events, because you can't have information about the future. As Keynes argued during the Great Depression, the future is not subject to risk but uncertainty, and "It would be foolish, in forming our expectations, to attach great weight to matters which are very uncertain."[19]

Any change is difficult to embrace and variables like commodity demand and supply are very difficult to understand, let alone predict. As much as you or I like to think of ourselves as forward-looking, the truth is that we are all backward-looking to some degree, and we update our perception of the world only gradually (something called adaptive expectations).

Take the example of oil. In the first few years of the 21st century, painful memories of the long period of low prices in the 1990s held back plans to expand production, even as prices surged. More recently, the production and investment plans of the major oil companies appear to have been based on the assumption that the period of high prices experienced between 2011 and mid-2014 would be sustained indefinitely. When prices have been high and rising for some time, it becomes an entrenched assumption that these high prices will persist for the foreseeable future and vice versa.[20]

In order to understand the demand or supply response in all commodities, it is important to realise that it is a joint function of prices, time and, finally, expectations. Prices are closely related to costs, and time is closely related to the delay in adjusting demand or supply to a change in the market. The important factor that is largely fuzzy is expectations. Expectations over future prices may begin to stabilise when the spot price volatility of a commodity falls, but may escalate in markets where the response of other producers or consumers is uncertain (see Chapter 7 on commodity cycles and Chapter 22 on commodity price volatility).

In the event that commodity prices rise, there may be a significant delay until production begins to respond. As explained in Chapter 7 the decision to invest in projects requiring large-scale investment (like developing a mine or an offshore oil field) are based on commodity prices assumed from feasibility studies and debt and equity raisings. These long-run commodity price assumptions tend to lag behind current commodity prices – strong evidence of adaptive expectations in action.

Price expectations are also important in determining demand over the longer-term period. High prices (and the threat, or at least the expectation, of even higher prices) affect both the consumer's behaviour and the investments by business. For oil, high and rising prices may spur substantial investment in fuel efficient vehicles and other equipment, as well as changes in behaviour and the substitution of cheaper fuels for oil.

The impact of high commodity prices may become deeply entrenched through the introduction of legislation. For example, it would very difficult to undo the US 2005 Energy Policy Act, the 2007 Energy Independence and Security Act and the Corporate Average Fuel Economy (CAFE) regulations.

Commodity markets have always operated this way. Instability and disequilibrium, rather than the opposite, are the norm.

The essential thing:

Price expectations influence both demand and supply.

9) Fossil fuels

"First rule of oil – addicts never tell the truth to their pushers. We are the addicts, the oil producers are the pushers – we've never had an honest conversation with the Saudis."

Thomas Friedman

First, a chemistry lesson! How much crude oil do you think comes from a brachiosaurus? The answer is zero. Oil formed from the remains of marine plants and animals that lived millions of years ago, long before dinosaurs roamed the planet. Bacterial decomposition of the plants and animals left behind a sludge mainly made of carbon and hydrogen, then pressure and heat changed the remaining compounds into hydrocarbons.[21] Today, these hydrocarbons take the form of gas, coal and oil and are the primary commodities used for heating, lighting and transportation in the global economy.

Oil

There are numerous varieties of crude oil, ranging from light or sweet to heavy or sour. The American Petroleum Institute measures how light or heavy the oils are, relative to water, in order to categorise them. As such, there is no one single oil price. Instead, different types of oil are generally priced at a premium or a discount according to significant benchmarks, including Brent and West Texas Intermediate (WTI), depending on their distance to market and their quality. Lighter oil generally commands a premium price because it is more suited to the production of petroleum in a refinery.

Typically found in underground or undersea reservoirs, crude oil is generally extracted using either the natural pressure in the reservoir or pumps. New extraction techniques, such as hydraulic fracturing and horizontal drilling, have been introduced as oil prices have increased and oil has become more complex and expensive to extract (see Chapter 36 on the shale revolution for more details).

Oil production tends to be concentrated in specific geographical regions, notably the Middle East, North and West Africa, the North Sea, North America and Russia. Many of the significant producers of oil are in geopolitically unstable regions. As such, output and, by extension, prices can be vulnerable to disruption due to strikes, civil unrest, resource nationalism or terrorist threats (you might want to see Chapter 27 and Chapter 28 for more discussion on why these factors represent an increasing risk).

Crude oil is not demanded for its own sake, but for the products or fuel types that can be derived from it. Crude oil offers more energy per kilogram than solid fuels like coal, and when compared with gases like Liquid Natural Gas (LNG) or propane it is much easier to handle. Crude oil can be refined into various products, such as light distillates (gasoline, naphtha etc.), middle distillates (jet and heating kerosene and gas and diesel oils) and fuel oils (including the oil used in maritime transport, otherwise called bunker). Energy accounts for the bulk of crude oil consumption, the largest consumers of which are transport and power generation. However, non-energy products that can also be produced from crude oil include solvents, petroleum coke, lubricants and bitumen.

The closest we, as consumers, get to the price of oil on a regular basis is the price of petrol or gasoline. An increase in the price of filling up your car can really hit your family's budget. What tends to fuel people's anger is when the cost is going up, yet the oil prices appear to be going down. However, think for a minute about the interactions that occur between the oil being pumped out of the ground and you putting fuel in your car.[22]

First, the pricing of crude oil itself is complicated (see Chapter 43). Before the black stuff is even out of the ground, its anticipated value has been traded on the futures market for weeks, months or even years. Second, there is the shipping market to get the stuff to shore (see Chapter 32). Highly volatile and as prone to geopolitical influences as oil itself, shipping deals are opaque because they are over-the-counter and are often based on long-term trading relationships.

Third, there are the refinery margins (also known as the crack spread) which represent the difference in price between the wholesale value of the products coming out of the refinery and the crude oil from which they were originally derived. This margin can be influenced by random factors including unscheduled refinery outages, workers on strike, storage costs and changes in the quality of the crude oil itself. Fourth, there is the cost of the transport from the refinery to the petrol station, competition between forecourts and the franchise owner's credit rating to account for. Fifth, and finally, after all of that the taxman must also have his share.

Gas

Gas tends to be found in underground rock beds (known as "non-associated" gas) or with other hydrocarbons (known as "associated" with oil or coal). Until the 1970s, "associated" gas was not considered to be commercially viable and was just burnt off or flared. Gas production tends to be concentrated in similar areas as oil – the Middle East and Russia, in particular. As technology has developed, it has become possible to extract gas from less accessible rock formations. These "unconventional" gases include tight gas (extracted from low-permeability rock formations) and shale gas (extracted from shale formations). This has led to higher gas output from other regions, most notably the US (see Chapter 36 on the shale revolution).

The electricity generation industry is by far the largest consumer of gas, followed by buildings (where gas is used to power boilers generating hot water and space heating) and industry (metal refining, petrochemicals, iron and steel). It is significantly easier to transport gas to people's homes than other fossil fuels, and it burns more cleanly. In contrast to oil, transportation is only a very small consumer of natural gas.

In contrast to many other commodities, gas does not have a global price benchmark. Instead, there are three distinct hubs in Asia, Europe and North America, represented by gas price benchmarks in Japan, the United Kingdom (UK) and the US. In part, this has been because of the difficulty in transporting gas over long distances. The continued growth in the LNG trade may, however, serve to change this over time and allow a global benchmark price for gas to evolve (see Chapter 32 for more discussion on LNG and the transportation of commodities in general).

Coal

Coal has been used as a source of energy for thousands of years, with evidence of its use in Ancient Greece, Imperial China and the Roman Empire. In the modern day, coal is still predominantly used in power generation. However, concerns over pollution have led many governments to try to reduce coal consumption, or at least slow the rate of increase (see Chapter 38).

Lignite is the lowest graded coal and is used exclusively in power plants (making up approximately 19% of coal reserves and with the lowest carbon content). Sub-bituminous and bituminous coal are the mid-grade coals used to make coke for steel making (making up approximately 80% of coal reserves). Anthracite is the highest graded coal and is typically used to heat buildings (making up approximately 1% of coal reserves and with the highest carbon content).

The essential thing:

Oil, gas and coal are fossil fuels, each with its own unique qualities.

Want to know more? Visit my blog **Materials Risk** *and get email updates and analysis on what's really happening in commodities and commodity markets.*

10) Low carbon energy

"We are like tenant farmers chopping down the fence around our house for fuel when we should be using Nature's inexhaustible sources of energy – sun, wind and tide. I'd put my money on the sun and solar energy. What a source of power! I hope we don't have to wait until oil and coal run out before we tackle that."

Thomas Edison

Renewable energy is nothing new. From wood for cooking and heating, wind to power ships and running water to drive cotton mills, much of the energy we consumed use to be from renewable sources. Renewable energy is generally defined as energy that comes from sources that are naturally replenished on a human timescale. Examples of renewable energy include: solar, wind, hydro, tidal, biomass and geothermal heat.

Solar

There are essentially two kinds of technology related to solar power. The first is photovoltaics (PV) which enable a beam of ultraviolet light to strike one half of a pair of negatively charged metal plates, freeing electrons which are then attracted to the other plate by electrostatic forces, generating an electrical current. The second technology is solar thermal, which concentrates sunlight on a heating fluid and is then converted to electricity via a steam generator.

In contrast to regular power stations, locality matters a great deal when harnessing solar power. During cloudless days on the equator, where the Earth's surface presents a plane that is perpendicular to the sun, the rays beat down at a maximum strength of 2,400 kW per m² per day. Estimates suggest that provided we could keep the sand off the panels, covering just 1% of the Sahara in solar panels (90,600 km² – an area slightly smaller than Portugal) would generate the same amount of electricity as all of the world's power stations in 2012 combined.[23]

The practical drawbacks from using solar power on such a scale, however, are considerable. The sun does not shine anywhere for 24 hours a day, nor does it shine much during the long winter months when our energy demand is greatest. Transporting that electricity to where it is needed most is costly and suffers from significant losses. And even if we can overcome these problems, scaling up solar power using PV will be hugely challenging, the reason being that PV cells produce electricity directly and there is currently no feasible, financially viable way to store it.

Wind

Wind power is the conversion of wind energy into a useful form of energy. Wind energy has been used to power ships and to generate the mechanical energy to power mills for hundreds of years. More recently, turbines have been used to produce electricity from wind.

Wind power is plentiful, renewable, widely distributed, clean, produces no greenhouse gas emissions during operation and uses little land. Wind power is very consistent from year to year, but has significant variation over shorter time scales. However, more than any other form of renewable energy, harnessing wind power has proved to be controversial. This is because of the need to place the wind turbines in areas that are exposed to the wind. They often need to be placed in otherwise unspoilt parts of the countryside, which can face plenty of opposition from local residents.

Hydropower

Hydroelectric power is harnessed through the gravitational force of falling or flowing water. The pressure generated as water passes through mechanical turbines is then converted into electricity. Hydroelectric power can be generated 24/7 indefinitely, assuming that the body of water it is utilising never runs dry.

Hydroelectric plants are very expensive to build and must be built to a very high standard. The high cost means that plants must operate for a long time before they become profitable.

The building of dams for hydroelectric power can cause a lot of water access problems. This is because the creation of a dam in one place may mean that those down river of the dam no longer have any control on water flow, creating problems for agriculture, in particular. This can also create controversy in places where neighbouring countries share a water supply. And the creation of dams also requires land to be flooded, which means the natural environment and the natural habitat of animals, and even people, may be destroyed.

Biomass/biofuel

We have harnessed biomass-derived energy since time began by burning wood. Biofuels are broadly classified into two major categories, based on the source of the biomass. First generation biofuels are derived from sources such as sugarcane and corn starch, etc. The sugars present in these biomass sources are fermented to produce bioethanol, an alcohol fuel which can be used directly in a fuel cell to produce electricity or can serve as an additive to gasoline. However, utilising food-based resources for fuel production may aggravate food shortage problems (see Chapter 16 for more details). Second generation biofuels, on the other hand, utilise non-food-based biomass sources, such as agriculture and municipal waste.[24]

Geothermal

Geothermal energy relates to the heat released deep from within the Earth's crust as a result of the radioactive decay of minerals and the ongoing heat loss following the original formation of the planet. Geothermal is a steady source of energy, has very high capacity utilisation rates, zero fuel costs, near zero greenhouse gas emissions and is suitable for both base load and flexible generation.

The Earth's geothermal resources are theoretically more than adequate to supply humanity's energy needs, but only a very small fraction may be profitably exploited.[25]

Nuclear

Not to be forgotten under the banner of low carbon power generation sources is nuclear power. It has the potential to help governments meet the stringent climate emission targets because, in contrast to many of the previously mentioned renewable energy sources, nuclear power can operate 24/7, 365 days of the year and generate a significant proportion of our energy needs. The most common fuel used in conventional nuclear fission power stations, uranium-235, is defined as being "non-renewable" according to the US Energy Information Administration (EIA).

The environmental and safety concerns of nuclear power have never been far away, however. On April 26th 1986, the Chernobyl nuclear power plant in Ukraine exploded, releasing large quantities of radioactive particles that spread across much of Europe and the then western Union of Soviet Socialist Republics (USSR). Then, in March 2011, one of the most powerful earthquakes in Japan's history and the subsequent tsunami resulted in a nuclear meltdown at the Fukushima Daiichi nuclear power plant, releasing radioactive material into the air and water.[26]

Renewable energy and commodity markets

What is the effect of more renewable energy on commodity markets? Although increased use of renewable energy should, all things being equal, lead to a decrease in demand for fossil fuels, it may lead to an increase in demand for other commodities that are required to deliver the renewable energy.

Rare earth metals, such as terbium, yttrium, dysprosium, europium and neodymium, are widely used in the manufacture of wind and wave turbines, solar panels and more broadly in electric car batteries and energy efficient light bulbs. A lack of supply of these rare metals, and many other critical raw materials, could threaten the development of renewable energy and increased energy efficiency (see more on this in Chapter 17).

An increase in the use of solar power may mean an increased demand for silver. This is because silver is a crucial component of solar panels and is used as a paste in manufacturing. Each crystalline silicon solar panel produced (approximately 85% of the market) uses the equivalent of 20 grams of silver per panel. According to the Silver Institute, approximately 80 tonnes of silver (2.8 million ounces) are needed to generate one gigawatt of electricity from solar sources. In 2013, almost 65 million ounces of silver were used in solar power generation, equating to 5%-10% of total silver demand.[27]

The essential thing:

Low carbon energy sources provide an alternative to, and a compliment to, the use of fossil fuels. However, they are not yet a "free lunch" and often come with significant costs of their own.

11) Ferrous metal

"The second technological innovation was the smelting and refining of metal, of which by far the most important was the making of iron followed later by steel."

Rod Beddows

Steel is the most ubiquitous metal, accounting for up 95% of global metal production. But where and for what is steel used for? Globally, construction accounts for approximately 50% of steel use. All economic activity requires construction, but the use of steel is more intensive at the earlier stages of development. For example, a distribution warehouse does not require the same amount of steel as a power plant, but it is still required in large quantities. Another 25% of steel goes into the manufacture of cars, domestic appliances, chemical products, etc, and the final 25% is used in consumer durables, anything from your laptop to your mobile phone and from tin cans to batteries.

China was responsible for approximately half of the global steel production in 2014. However, in the same year annual growth in Chinese steel production slowed to its lowest level since 1990 as Chinese policymakers looked to diversify their economy away from investment, and towards consumption. The main consumers of steel in China are property, machinery, infrastructure, automobiles and appliances, with property being bigger than the other four sectors combined.

Steel is categorised as being a ferrous metal, meaning that it mostly comprises iron. Non-ferrous metals, like copper, aluminium and zinc, do not contain iron (to learn more see Chapter 12 on base metals and Chapter 13 on precious metals). Despite its importance to the global economy, iron ore – the essential raw material from which steel is made – attracts relatively little attention.[28]

The trade in iron ore is the second-largest commodity market by value after crude oil, but it is worth less than a tenth of the $3 trillion of crude traded every year. Iron ore lacks the clout of oil for several reasons. In contrast to oil, iron is plentiful. It makes up 5% of the Earth's crust and is the fourth most abundant element after oxygen, silicon and aluminium. The difficulty is finding it in sufficient concentrations and then shifting the millions of tonnes of ore to where it is needed.[29]

In contrast to oil and many other commodities, iron ore is also largely a physical market, ie, generally free from speculative money. Up until 2003, iron ore prices were based on a long-term benchmark price system that involved both the largest iron ore miners and Japanese steelmakers agreeing on the price. The system worked because global steel production grew only slowly and iron ore prices did not change very much. However, as China became an increasing presence in the iron ore market, the existing system – which had lasted for over 40 years – was no longer tenable. In 2010, the big miners abandoned the benchmark and began to sell their ore on short-term contracts, at prices set on a nascent spot market.

Iron ore is present in the form of rocks and minerals from which the ore can be extracted. It is found in the form of hematite and magnetite deposits, although goethite, limonite and siderite deposits are also common. These deposits vary with the percentage of the iron content present. More content means better quality ore, less cost and less time consumed during the iron ore extraction.[30]

Hematite has the highest iron ore content of 70%. This type of deposit is most abundant in Brazil, Australia and some parts of Asia (mainly China and the surrounding areas). Prior to the industrial revolution, most of the iron ore was mined directly from hematite deposits. However, rising demand for the ore and depleting hematite deposits led to the development of methods to extract low-grade iron ore sources, like magnetite and goethite.

Australia and Brazil currently dominate the seaborne trade in iron ore, with a 72% market share. Although China is the largest producer of iron ore, it's also the largest importer, followed by Japan and Europe.[31]

Once extracted, the ore goes through a concentration process that removes impurities and increases the iron content. Next, the beneficiation process improves its physical properties and makes the ore more usable. An iron-rich clinker call sinter is formed when this ore is mixed with coke and heated. Coke, ore and sinter are then put into a blast furnace, together with limestone. The hot air blast separates the iron, which collects at the bottom of the furnace in its molten form. This is pig iron, which is processed further by removing carbon and adding steel scrap (ie steel that has been previously used and is now available to be recycled) and other metals – according to the nature and purpose for which the final product will be used – to form steel.

Steel is 100% recyclable. More than 1,400 kg of iron ore, 740 kg of coal and 120 kg of limestone are saved for every tonne of steel scrap made into new steel. In addition, each tonne of recycled steel uses 40% less water, 75% less energy, generates 1.28 tonnes less solid waste, emits 86% less air emissions and 76% less water pollution than steel from raw materials. Steel can be manufactured using two types of furnace: a blast furnace or an electric arc furnace. Blast furnace operators use around 25% steel scrap as input, this compares with electric arc furnaces that use approximately 80% steel scrap (see Chapter 18 on secondary commodities).[32, 33]

The essential thing:

Steel production makes up almost all of the global metal output and steel is made primarily from iron ore, one of the most underappreciated commodities.

12) Base metals

"But that's because Dr Copper is a fictional creation, a neat way for market commentators to distil a complex industrial market into a one-dimensional character."

Andy Home

Base metals refer to all non-ferrous metals, excluding precious metals. Base metals are more abundant and so less expensive than precious metals like gold and platinum (see Chapter 13). Because of this, as well as their unique utilities, base metals are widely used in commercial and industrial applications. The main base metals are aluminium and copper, with zinc, lead, tin and nickel used to a lesser extent.

Aluminium

Aluminium is the most abundant metallic element in the Earth's crust. It is found in large quantities in bauxite, an ore that contains aluminium oxide or alumina. Bauxite typically contains approximately 30-35% aluminium and is mined primarily in tropical parts of the world. Alumina is extracted from the bauxite ore in a refinery using the Bayer process, and is then smelted to produce primary aluminium.[34, 35]

As a general rule of thumb, four-five tonnes of bauxite produce approximately two tonnes of alumina, which generates one tonne of aluminium. The production of aluminium is highly energy intensive (approximately 14,000 kWh of electricity is needed to produce one tonne of aluminium) with the result that many smelters are in energy-rich countries.

Aluminium is lightweight but strong, and these qualities are making it an increasingly attractive alternative to steel, particularly in cars. Its other properties include good conductivity, resistance to corrosion, elasticity and a low melting point (which makes it easily recyclable). It has a wide range of end uses in, for example, electronics, transport (particularly aircraft and vehicles), construction, cooking utensils and food packaging.

Copper

Within the manufacturing sectors, copper is widely used in machinery and is also turned into end products and semi-manufactures like pipes and tubes. Because it acts as an effective conductor of heat and electricity, copper is also used in the installation, energy and telecommunications sectors. As a good conductor of heat, it is also widely used in the transport equipment industry – a passenger car contains approximately 20-50 kg of copper and approximately 1 km of copper wires and cables.[36]

The production of copper is capital-intensive and dominated by three components: the price and quality of raw materials, the energy costs and the labour costs. The refining of copper is above all an energy intensive process. Energy costs account for approximately 30% of the total cost of extracting the ore, and these costs can rise to 50% during the processing of the ores (smelting and refining). When the oil price rises, energy costs will go up, and the copper price may rise too.

Given its ubiquitous use, copper is often referred to as "Doctor Copper" with trends in the copper market often thought to be a useful indicator of the state of the world's economy. In theory, when demand for copper grows its price will rise. Therefore, greater demand for copper means that industrial activity is rising and, hence, that the economy is expanding. But is there any sense in this?

The link between world trade and copper price movements is strong. Given that production and consumption of metals generally take place in different parts of the world, global trade in ores and refined metals (by land or sea) is unavoidable. When the copper price falls, this may point to a fall in demand, and consequently a decline in global trade in dry bulk goods.

All of this ignores that all commodities are a function of supply, as well as demand. Copper's sensitivity to demand is accurate only if you assume that supply is a constant, miraculously rising and falling to match consumption at all times. In the short term, the copper price (and other metal prices) is affected by investor sentiment as well as other factors (such as the use of copper as collateral), which means that significant price fluctuations can occur even though there is no reason for such volatility on pure fundamental grounds.

The others - zinc, lead, tin and nickel

Zinc is used mainly in galvanising, die casting and brass (alloyed with copper), which together account for approximately 80% of its use. It is also used to a lesser extent in batteries, chemicals and rubber. Galvanising (the process of applying a protective zinc coating to steel to prevent rusting) is by far the largest market for zinc accounting for about 45% of total zinc demand with the construction industry the largest consumer of galvanised steel. Transport accounts for approximately 25% of zinc demand with consumer goods and electrical appliances at 23% and general engineering at approximately 7%.

Lead is one of the scarcer non-ferrous metals in the Earth's crust. Lead has many useful properties; in particular, it is highly resistant to corrosion and it is malleable, melting and joining easily. Its high density makes it a valuable insulating material for electrical and radiation screening and soundproofing. The electrochemical properties of lead make it a useful component in storage batteries in motor vehicles and for some back-up power supplies. According to the International Lead and Zinc Study Group, lead use in battery manufacture now accounts for approximately 80% of total consumption, compared with approximately 30% in the 1960s.

An increasing awareness of the toxicity of lead has led to changes in the pattern of lead consumption. The first and most high profile change took place in the 1980s, when lead was progressively removed from automotive fuels. For the same reason, there has also been a decline in the use of lead in paints, solders and ammunition.

Tin is one of the earliest metals known to man. During the Bronze Age, tin was added to copper to make bronze – the addition of tin makes the copper stronger and easier to cast. Tin has a low melting point, is malleable and resistant to corrosion and it alloys readily with other metals. It is also non-toxic and easy to recycle, attributes that have become increasingly important. The main use of tin is in solder alloys, which are widely used to attach components to circuit boards used in the manufacture of electronic equipment and electrical appliances and for joining pipes in plumbing systems.

Nickel's main use is as an alloy with chrome in stainless steel. It has ideal characteristics for this given that it is resistant to corrosion and can be given a high polish. The main sources of nickel are Russia, the Philippines and Indonesia (see Chapter 35 on recent innovation in nickel production).

The essential thing:

Base metals are used throughout the economy, with copper prices in particular often seen as a signal of impending changes in global economic growth.

*Want to know more? Visit my blog **Materials Risk** and get email updates and analysis on what's really happening in commodities and commodity markets.*

13) Precious metals

"I know of only two men who really understand the value of gold, an obscure clerk in the basement vault of the Banque de France and one of the directors of the Bank of England.

"Unfortunately, they disagree."

N.M. Rothschild

Gold bug. That's the term used to describe those investors who have an almost religious zeal for the shiny gold metal. At a basic level, a precious metal is a rare, naturally occurring metal of high economic value. But to many, it's much more than that. The most widely known precious metal is gold. Other precious metals include silver and the platinum group of metals (PGMs), such as ruthenium, rhodium, palladium, osmium, iridium and platinum.

Although all of the precious metals have at least some practical uses – from jewellery to industrial applications – gold stands out from the others because its demand is primarily driven by investment and as a store of value. Gold is not like any other commodity, therefore. Gold has no significant remaining uses as a producer good because equivalent or superior alternatives exist for all of its industrial uses. As an example, although approximately 70 tonnes of gold are used in dentistry annually, it is gradually giving way to advanced composites and porcelain veneers and crowns.

Of course, Gold is used for jewellery. But even in countries like India, where gold jewellery is very popular, the metal is historically used as a form of investment and financial security for married woman. Therefore, households tend to increase their purchases when prices fall, and vice versa when they rise. Indeed, changes in demand from households in these significant markets can influence gold prices (see Chapter 6 for how rainfall in India can affect the demand for gold).

Gold is also anonymous, in the sense that it is accepted as payment without the receiving party having to know the identity of the paying party. This can only work, however, if something can be reliably identified as being or not being gold.[37]

Gold is a "fiat commodity" – one that has value as an asset if and to the extent that enough people believe that it has value. Like paper, currency gold is "irredeemable". It is an "outside" asset – an asset of the holder that is not a liability of anyone else. As a fiat commodity currency, gold's value will be largely determined by its attractiveness relative to other fiat currencies – the fiat paper currencies issued by central banks. In this way, gold should not be analysed in the same way as just another intrinsically valuable commodity (silver, iron, lead, zinc, platinum, aluminium, titanium, etc.), but as part of a set of fiat currencies – the US dollar, the Euro, etc. Gold will be most attractive when market participants are most nervous about the future value of other fiat currencies. And concern among investors tends to grow when governments appear to be spending too much (ie, increasing the size of their budget deficit) and/or when central banks do not do enough to contain rising prices. Inflation, of course, acts to erode the purchasing value of currency.

Gold is just a shiny metal. There is little intrinsic to gold that enables it to serve as a store of value and a hedge against inflation. Gold serves these purposes only because people assign it with the ability to do so. Many view gold as a lot like religion. No one can prove that God exists; either you are a believer or you're not. The same can be said for gold. By investing in gold you are taking a view as to whether other people's faith in gold will increase or erode.

Gold and other precious metals are often used as a hedge against uncertainty, and geopolitical uncertainty in particular. Gold prices peaked in 1980 at $850 per oz when the Soviet Union invaded Afghanistan, which also coincided with the Iranian hostage crisis at the US Embassy in Tehran. The rise to 2011's record peak of $1,920 per oz came as several of the Arab Spring revolutions descended into civil war and Greece was brought to a standstill by a general strike against the Eurozone's austerity demands.[38]

Before the introduction of fiat currency, precious metals and gold, in particular, were used as a means of exchange and a way of storing value and protecting the purchasing power of an individual against inflation. The first use of gold as a means of exchange dates back to approximately 600 BC in Asia Minor (present day Turkey). More recently the Bretton Woods Agreements established a system, after World War II, in which many countries fixed their exchange rates relative to the US dollar, and central banks could exchange dollar holdings into gold at the official exchange rate of $35 per oz.[39]

Central banks and governments may also affect the price of gold, in particular through changes in the reserves of the precious metals that they hold. As of September 2015, central banks and other organisations held 32,682.4 tonnes of gold as official gold reserves, 21% of the gold ever mined. Central banks may sometimes look to off load or top up their gold reserves. One example of particularly bad timing was the decision by the UK government to sell off approximately half of its gold reserves between 1999 and 2002, when gold prices were at their lowest for 20 years. The UK achieved an average price of $275 per oz.[40]

The cost and waste involved in getting the gold out of the ground only to put it back under ground in secure vaults is considerable - whether for central banks as part of their foreign exchange reserves or for gold held idle in private vaults as a store of value. Indeed, as economist Willem Buiter argues the entire gold supply chain - from mining, refining and its storage - is a socially wasteful activity.[41]

Most of the gold ever mined still exists in accessible form and is thus potentially able to come back onto the gold market for the right price. At the end of 2006, it was estimated that all the gold ever mined amounted to 158,000 tonnes, enough to fit into a 20 m x 20 m cube. Given the huge quantity of gold stored above ground compared to the annual production (~2,500 tonnes), the price of gold is mainly affected by changes in sentiment (demand), rather than changes in annual production (supply).

Precious metals don't always stay precious, however. An initially precious metal that later became common was aluminium. Although aluminium is the most abundant metal in the Earth's crust, it was at first exceedingly difficult to extract from its various non-metallic ores. Until relatively recently, the great expense of refining aluminium made the small available quantity of pure aluminium more valuable than gold. Indeed, when Napoleon III of France reigned in the 1850s, his most important guests were given aluminium cutlery, whereas those less worthy dined with mere gold. At the time, aluminium was worth approximately $1,200 per kg, whereas gold was half that. Over time, however, the price of the metal has dropped and now aluminium is only in demand for its industrial uses (see Chapter 12).[42]

The essential thing:

Gold is a *fiat* commodity.

14) Agriculture

"We not only need to grow an extra one billion tonnes of cereals a year by 2050… but do so from a diminishing resource base of land and water in many of the world's regions, and in an environment increasingly threatened by global warming and climate change."

Jacques Diouf, Director General, Food and Agriculture Organization of the United Nations (FAO)

Agricultural commodities are essentially those that are grown from the ground. Like other commodities, they are not consumed in their primary form but undergo a process of refining and processing so that they can be used as ingredients to make food (eg, corn) and drinks (eg, coffee and sugar), and as materials to make products like clothing (eg, cotton) and tyres (eg, rubber).

Rice, wheat and corn vie for the position of most important agricultural commodity. Rice is responsible for more than a fifth of all the calories consumed by humans, making it our most eaten crop. Wheat is the crop that covers more of the Earth than any other crop, while also being the leading source of vegetable proteins. Meanwhile, corn (known as maize in some parts of the world) has the largest global production, although not all of it is eaten by humans.[43]

Corn

Corn is a cereal grain that has been grown since prehistoric times. Corn is the most widely grown crop in the world, with almost half the world's corn produced in the US. Between them, the US, China, Brazil, Mexico, Argentina, India and France produce over three-quarters of the world's corn.

Approximately 60% of the corn grown is used for animal feed, with human consumption typically accounting for approximately 11%. The remainder is used by industry, mainly for ethanol and starch (see Chapter 16 on biofuel's demand for corn and other agricultural commodities).

Rice

Rice thrives in areas with heavy rainfall. The traditional method of cultivation involves flooding the fields with water (paddies), which helps to repel weeds and pests. It is usually an annual crop, but in some countries (India, for example) a winter and a summer crop can be sown. In several countries in Asia, rice farming is coming under pressure from urbanisation and competition from other crops, but the use of high yielding or disease resistant varieties has allowed production to grow.

There are many varieties of rice, but almost all are grown for human consumption, which accounts for approximately 90% of (milled) production. Some lower-quality rice and surpluses that cannot be marketed may be sold for animal feed.

Wheat

The cultivation of wheat was essential in enabling the emergence of many city-based societies at the start of civilisation. Originating in the Fertile Crescent close to modern day Syria and Iraq, wheat was one of the first crops that could be easily cultivated on a large scale. Because of its ability to cope with a wide range of weather conditions, it is now grown throughout the world. There are wide variations in global yields, however. Higher protein hard wheats, which are grown in a short summer season under relatively dry conditions, suffer lower yields than other types. Meanwhile varieties grown for animal feed tend to have higher yields.

The export price of the US' number two Hard Red Winter wheat is usually taken as the global benchmark because the wheat is always available and widely traded. Durum (for pasta) and high protein wheats are more expensive, whereas soft varieties for biscuit making are cheaper. Prices of feed grade wheats, meanwhile, are usually aligned with feed barley and corn.[44]

Soybeans

The most important global crop for livestock is soybeans. Soy is a legume which produces beans containing high levels of protein and oil. The harvested beans are processed to extract the oil (approximately 20% of the bean), which is used primarily as a vegetable cooking oil or a food ingredient. The high protein soymeal that is left over after oil extraction is toasted and ground and is used mainly for animal feed, particularly for cattle, pigs or poultry. The Food and Agriculture Organization of the United Nations (FAO) estimates that for every tonne of soybean oil, 4.5 tonnes of soybean meal are produced.

Soybean cultivation is highly concentrated: four countries – the US, Brazil, Argentina and China – account for most of the world's output (86% in 2011). Historically, the US was by far the largest producer and exporter of soybeans, but there has been significant expansion of production in Latin America, Brazil and Argentina.

Cotton

Not all crops are grown to be eaten. Cotton, wool and rubber are some of the major non-food agricultural commodities that are globally traded. Although cotton competes with other natural fibres (such as wool, flax, jute and bamboo), more serious competition has come from synthetic petroleum-based fibres (such as polyester) and artificial, cellulose-based fibres (including rayon and acetate).

Approximately 60% of cotton consumption is in the manufacture of clothing, notably jeans, shirts and t-shirts. A significant proportion is used to make household textiles: towels, table linen, bedding, curtains and upholstery fabrics. Cotton accounted for an estimated one-third of the world's fibre consumption in 2010, compared with almost half in 1990. In many products – woven shirts, for example – cotton is often now blended, usually with polyester.

China is the world's largest producer of cotton, accounting for nearly 27.4% of global output, but India is not far behind with a 21.5% market share (the control of cotton supply has been a significant geopolitical concern in the past, see Chapter 28).[45]

Rubber

The tyre industry is by far the world's largest consumer of natural rubber, accounting for an estimated 70% of consumption. As well as tyres, a modern automobile has more than 300 components made out of rubber. It is also used to make conveyor belts, footwear, medical instruments, hoses and floor coverings etc.

Rubber trees originated in Latin America. During the colonial period, the British took seeds from Brazil, via the UK, to Singapore, India, Sri Lanka and British Malaya, and Belgian colonists took seeds to what is now the Democratic Republic of Congo. Today, Asia accounts for approximately 90% of total production. The three largest producers – Thailand, Indonesia and Malaysia – accounted for 67% of global production in 2011.

The essential thing:

Agricultural crops are grown for food, feed, fuel and fibre.

15) Livestock

"You can't just turn cows on and off."

Kevin Bellamy, Rabobank

"The advance and decline in the value of hogs to be for twenty years past... as... certain as the diurnal revolutions of the earth upon its axis."

Samual Brenner

Livestock feed on one-third of the world's crops and are a commodity in their own right. The demand for meat is closely linked to a country's economic development, with richer consumers generally consuming a greater amount of meat in their diets. Urbanisation and rising incomes mean that more of the world is converging on European and American levels of meat consumption, which is approximately 100 kg a year per person. At the moment, most of Africa and South Asia eats less than 20 kg of meat a year per person.

Cattle (beef), pigs (pork) and chickens (poultry) are the three main categories of livestock that are raised for human consumption. Livestock are generally fed on grains like corn, soybeans, barley and sorghum. In general, beef is the more expensive meat relative to chicken and pork. Since chicken and pigs convert 1 kg of feed into 2-4 times as much body mass than a cow, it makes producing poultry and pork less expensive than beef.[46]

If feed grain prices increase (so that total input costs rise), the cost of raising livestock also goes up, reducing margins for farmers. Rather than feed cows, pigs and chickens at flat to negative operating margins, livestock owners may opt to slaughter more of their herd instead.[47] In the short term this then supplies the market with excess meat and drives prices even lower. But in the long term, equilibrium in operating margins is restored by either a greater supply of feed grains driving input prices down or decreased livestock production increasing market prices.

Conversely, if feed prices decline, it costs less to feed livestock for each additional pound of gain. This lower cost makes it more profitable to continue feeding animals for longer and thus creates a short-term reduction in livestock supply to the market. The expected long-term increase in supply will not appear for a time equal to the length of the feeding period for each animal. This is because when feed prices decline, livestock feeders buy more young animals to increase their feeding herd size. However, it is not until these animals are fed to slaughter weight that the increase in supply is realised.

In general, cattle prices follow a broadly predictable pattern known as the "hog cycle" which lasts approximately 10-12 years (a similar pattern is observed in other forms of livestock). Increasing cattle prices spur producers to retain female animals to increase the breeding herd, at first reducing slaughter numbers and, as a result, increasing prices further. However, once these female animals begin producing offspring and these in turn eventually reach slaughter weight, there may be an oversupply of livestock. Prices then begin to decline and it eventually becomes unprofitable to raise and feed young cattle. Producers then begin culling the breeding herd and sending them to slaughter, adding additional numbers to the supply and causing prices to decrease even further (see Chapter 8 for more on how expectations affect supply).

Just as the product produced from eating crops (livestock) can be called a commodity, the produce that these livestock then produce is also often termed a commodity; for instance, the supply of dairy products is very much linked to herd numbers. A range of dairy products are traded as commodities, including butter, cheese and a range of different milk powders. The products are commonly traded on exchanges in New Zealand and the US.

Meat has a big environmental hoof-print. It accounts for 17% of global calorie intake, but it uses twice as much grain, land and water to fatten an animal to produce a pound of meat than it does to grow the same number of calories in the form of a grain that is eaten directly. More land is given over to grazing animals than for any other single purpose. Approximately a third of the world's crops are fed to animals, and they also use a third of all available freshwater. Animals also belch and fart remarkable quantities of greenhouse gases, accounting for between 8% and 18% of global emissions. The amount of greenhouse gases associated with the production of a kilo of protein varies widely by different animals: 3.7 kg for chicken, 24 kg for pork and up to 1,000 kg for cattle (see Chapter 38 on climate change).[48,49]

Could insects provide an alternative animal feed of the future? The Food and Agriculture Organization of the United Nations (FAO) published a report in 2013 promoting the introduction of insects into both our diets and animal feed. The potential to reduce demand for grains and the impact on the environment could be significant (see Chapter 41 on sustainable commodities). Nevertheless, you might agree with me that a hamburger that comes from a pig reared on insect feed is likely to be more palatable than a burger bun made from cricket flour.[50]

The essential thing:

Livestock is the biggest land user in the world, feeding on one-third of the world's crops.

Want to know more? Visit my blog **Materials Risk** *and get email updates and analysis on what's really happening in commodities and commodity markets.*

16) Biofuels

"Tortillas si, Pan no!"

Mexican food protest chant

On January 31st 2007, large crowds built in Mexico City, incensed by the quadrupling in the price of corn (the main ingredient in tortillas) over the previous few months. Citizens, farmers and union activists joined forces in what became known as the tortilla riots. Many commentators believe that the fuse that lit their indignation was sparked two years previously, by an apparently disconnected event. In August 2005, Hurricane Katrina caused the shutdown of almost all of the oil and gas production in the US Gulf for several months, resulting in a surge in the price of gasoline in America (see Chapter 9 on fossil fuels).

This spike in oil prices made corn – the primary ingredient in the alternative fuel ethanol – look relatively cheap by comparison and spurred investment in domestic ethanol production. Concerned by US energy security, Congress mandated a fivefold increase in biofuel production – with more than 40% of it to come from corn. Between 2005 and 2011, the grain used to produce fuel for cars climbed from 41 million to 127 million tons – nearly a third of the US grain harvest.[51]

This wasn't the first time that the idea of growing crops for fuel seemed to be a good idea. At the time of the Arab oil export embargo in the 1970s, major oil importing countries asked themselves if there were alternatives to oil. In a number of countries, particularly the US, several in Europe, and Brazil, the idea of growing crops for fuel began to take hold. Indeed, even further back, Henry Ford's Model T ran on both ethanol and petroleum – Ford believing that biofuels were the "fuel of the future".

The expansion in biofuel production, and hence demand for crops such as corn, has been driven by a number of economic and environmental factors. First, reducing a nation's dependence on high energy prices may help improve its energy security, leaving it less vulnerable to disruption. And second, environmental concerns related to the consumption of fossil fuels. Governmental policies have sought to accelerate this transition through mandates, tax credits and other policies aimed at increasing energy efficiency and reducing emissions.

Diverting food crops into biofuel production can raise the price of food. This happens directly via competition for the same grain between food, feed and biofuel users, but also indirectly, by diverting land away from other agricultural commodities. Soybeans are the crop most directly affected by the demand for corn-based ethanol, because corn and soybeans tend to compete for land area.

With certain agricultural commodities now seen as substitutes to oil, this allows the transmission of higher oil prices and volatility to affect agricultural prices directly. You can quickly see that the diversion of one crop (corn for example) from food to biofuel, combined with higher and volatile oil prices, can rapidly affect output and prices right across the agricultural supply chain – impacting the price of food that you and I buy every day.

The increased demand for corn for making biofuels following Hurricane Katrina was a boon for US corn farmers, of course. But, as participants in the tortilla riots in Mexico City found out to their cost, not so for many less developed economies that now had to import corn and other agricultural commodities at much higher prices.

I should make clear that the use of corn as a biofuel is just one of a number of factors that resulted in corn and other food prices spiking at the time. As other chapters in this book highlight, stock levels, the weather, demographics, production costs, exchange rates and resource nationalism, amongst others, can all affect commodity prices. And there is still uncertainty as to the weight that each factor has in a particular episode of rising agricultural prices.

Bearing this in mind then, if the use of crops like corn and other biomass at least helps to drive up their price alongside fossil fuels, then one of the arguments for relying on crops as fuel starts to look a bit shaky. But what about the other problems with devoting more land to the production of biofuels?

First, biofuel production increases competition for land. Approximately three-quarters of the world's vegetated land are used to produce food and forest products. Much of the rest contains natural ecosystems that keep climate-warming carbon out of the atmosphere, protect freshwater supplies and preserve biodiversity. Diverting land – even degraded, under-utilised areas – to bioenergy means sacrificing much needed food, timber and carbon storage.

Second, bioenergy production is an inefficient use of land. Although photosynthesis may do a great job of converting the sun's rays into food, it is an inefficient way to turn solar radiation into non-food energy that people can use. Research suggests that bioenergy could meet 20% of the world's total annual energy demand by 2050. Yet doing so would require feedstock equal to all of the world's current crop harvests, plant residues, timber and grass consumed by livestock.[52,53]

Third, and finally, bioenergy does not generally cut greenhouse gas emissions. Burning biomass, whether directly as wood or in the form of ethanol or biodiesel, emits carbon dioxide just like burning fossil fuels. In fact, burning biomass directly emits more carbon dioxide than fossil fuels for the same amount of generated energy.

The essential thing:

Turning food into a fuel can have unintended consequences, and its environmental benefits may not be quite as a good as they seem.

17) Rare earth elements

"There is oil in the Middle East; there is rare earth in China."

Deng Xiaoping

During 2010 and into 2011, the price of obscure metals with strange names like terbium, dysprosium and europium went stratospheric, with some multiplying tenfold. The spark for this price surge? China had increased export tariffs and reduced export quotas in an apparent attempt to give its domestic electronics manufacturing industries a competitive advantage, by ensuring them a cheap, captive supply of these essential raw materials.

So what's so important about these obscure metals? Well, rare earth elements (REEs) are highly sought-after chemical elements that are essential components of a wide range of products, from smartphones to wind turbines and cancer-treating drugs. The 17 recognised REEs are all used widely, although each has specialised applications, including: oil refining, electronics (in headphones, smartphones and cameras), transportation (in hybrid and electric cars), phosphors (in lighting and television/computer screens), catalysts (in catalytic converters within engines), defence (in lasers and jets) and green energy (in wind turbines).

Most products only need a very small amount of REEs, but they are vital for production. For example, there are still no known substitutes for europium and terbium in producing the red and green colours in a television screen. Products that need most REEs include hybrid cars, jets engines and wind turbines. For example, a typical hybrid car uses approximately 30 kg of REEs, mainly as magnets in the electric motors, and the permanent magnet used to operate a three megawatt (medium-sized) wind turbine contains approximately two tonnes of REEs.

Despite their name, "rare" earth elements are actually more abundant than some base and precious metals. However, it is usually hard to find a commercially viable quantity in any one place, and they are difficult, expensive and environmentally unfriendly to mine and refine. Global REE production generally involves two phases: mining and processing (with varying levels of processing required depending on the end use). REE mines take source material from the ground, use physical and chemical differences between the REE containing minerals and other minerals to concentrate the product and then separate out the first material, known as rare earth oxides. These oxides are then converted into rare earth metals, which are often then combined with other metals to form alloys.

REEs can be roughly divided into two categories: light (lower atomic number) and heavy (higher atomic number). In general, heavy REEs are less readily available than light REEs and this is reflected in the price, with heavy REEs, like dysprosium and terbium, being generally more expensive.

Until the 1990s, the US was the dominant producer of REEs and China mined almost none. That changed after the largest US mine, Mountain Pass, shut in the wake of complaints about environmental damage and the high level of capital investment required. Chinese producers took advantage of cheap labour and more relaxed environmental regulations to ramp up production. By 2010, China supplied 97% of the global market.[54]

The spike in prices in 2010/2011 also brought attention to the geopolitical risk of REEs because of their use in strategically important products such as defence systems, jet engines, wind turbines and electric cars.[55] To adapt an old saying in other commodity markets, the cure for high REE prices is high REE prices. The spike in prices incentivised output to expand elsewhere, new sources were discovered and manufacturers found ways to economise on REEs or found substitutes. By mid-2015, China was still the main producer of REEs, accounting for approximately 85% of global production, yet REE prices have since fallen all the way back to levels seen before the trade restrictions were implemented.[56]

The recovery and recycling of REEs is another option to increase supply. However, REEs are difficult to extract from used electronic equipment and then recycle economically. As with other commodities, but particularly REEs, designing products with repair and reuse in mind can prolong the lifetime of REE consumption.

In contrast to most of the other commodity markets outlined in this part of the book, REEs do not trade on a futures exchange, although daily Chinese spot price data is available for most REEs. From an investor's perspective, at present, the only way to gain exposure to REEs is to invest in the shares of REE miners based outside of China (see Chapter 46 on how to invest in commodities).

The essential thing:

Rare earth elements (REEs) are essential components for a wide range of technologies, from wind turbines and military defence systems, to your smartphone.

18) Secondary commodities

"Today's goods are tomorrow's resources at yesterday's prices."

Walter Stahel

What alternative routes are there to extracting materials other than digging them out of the ground or growing them? Well, you could always recover them and then recycle them into new products. As well as reducing the need for virgin (newly dug out of the ground/grown) commodities, recycling materials can also result in significant energy savings. Recycling aluminium, for example, requires 96% less energy and produces 95% fewer greenhouse gas emissions than manufacturing virgin aluminium. A number of terms are used to describe the various materials/commodities that are collected, from "scrap" to "recovered materials", but throughout this chapter I will use the term "secondary commodities".[57]

Metal recycling has been carried out for centuries. In pre-industrial times, there is evidence of bronze and other metals being collected in Europe and then melted down for perpetual reuse. Both ferrous and non-ferrous metals see little or no degradation during the recycling process and so can be recycled indefinitely. According to estimates from the International Copper Study Group (ICSG), more than 30% of global copper consumption comes from copper scrap, with other metals typically consuming similar proportions of scrap.[58]

The long lifespan of many metal products means that the amount of metal available for recycling cannot keep up with the global demand growth for new products. With steel, structures can last 60 years or more and cars often last longer than 12 years. Steel products can be seen as scrap-in-inventory, meaning that the steel will not be ready for recycling until the long life of the product comes to an end.

More recently, attention has concentrated on the recycling of other secondary commodities that are in our waste stream but also have value: paper, plastic, metal cans and glass to name just a few. But not all secondary commodities are made equally. Whereas metal, glass and plastic can be recycled indefinitely, other materials like paper gradually deteriorate as the fibres shorten.

Secondary commodities may exhibit many of the characteristics of other commodity markets, but one significant issue where they differ is on the matter of fungibility (see Chapter 1). One of the basic characteristics of a commodity is that it should be uniform in quality and lacking in product differentiation, meaning that the market treats its instances as equivalent, or nearly so, with no regard to who produced them. For secondary commodities, the issue of quality may have a significant impact on the price; for example, if different materials are mixed together (say glass and paper) the quality may suffer, or if they are exposed to the elements the moisture content might increase. The result is that in contrast to primary commodity markets, it's much more difficult to price a secondary commodity, with the range of prices quoted at any one time likely to be wide.

The main factor affecting the price of secondary commodities is the underlying virgin commodity prices and the extent to which the former are seen as substitutes for the latter. For example, if demand for aluminium increases, leading to higher virgin aluminium prices, then the demand for scrap aluminium should also rise, leading to higher scrap aluminium prices. However, secondary commodities are generally priced at a discount to virgin commodities, reflecting that their quality may not be as good or as consistent as virgin supplies and that they are probably from a more unstable and less secure source.

Sometimes secondary commodities can be affected by developments in other commodities in very unusual and indirect ways. Take the humble soft drink or water bottle, made out of polyethylene terephthalate (PET). PET isn't just used for packaging, it also competes with cotton in the production of clothing and other textiles. Many recovered PET bottles are exported to China and other economies in Asia, in order to be used in the production of polyester. As they are seen as substitutes in fibre production when cotton prices go up, so PET prices may also go up.

A range of other factors also affects the market for secondary commodities. This may include government regulation, the supply of secondary commodities (ie, how much is collected) from the waste stream and the demand for recycled commodities.

Markets for secondary commodities are diverse. Heavier, low value secondary commodities, like glass, tend to only be transported short distances. In Europe, for example, glass is often exported back to wine producing countries like Portugal for reprocessing. Higher value secondary commodities, like paper and plastic, are traded globally much like virgin commodities. Here China is a significant end market, with buyers often identifying the materials they need based on movements in exchange rates, shipping times and concerns over quality. Container ships used to transport the goods that China produces for markets in Europe, North America and other countries then carry the recovered paper and plastic back to China on the "backhaul" voyage.

In contrast to virgin commodities, the supply of secondary commodities is essentially fixed in the short-term; it being dependent on the consumption of products and then its subsequent recovery as a secondary commodity. If you demand more of a particular secondary commodity, then you either have to hope that more is collected from the waste stream or that people consume more of the product providing the secondary commodities you require in the first place. With supply of secondary commodities being very price inelastic, an increase in demand may mean prices increase sharply and vice versa in the event of declining demand (see Chapter 22).

Further contributing to the level of volatility is that many secondary commodities can be difficult to store, resulting in low stock levels. For instance, paper may become damp if not stored correctly, and government regulations may prevent companies from holding too much of a particular material, say plastic, because of the risk of fire.

The essential thing:

Secondary commodities represent an alternative source of commodities.

Want to know more? Visit my blog **Materials Risk** *and get email updates and analysis on what's really happening in commodities and commodity markets.*

19) Commodity prices and the economy

"In economics things take longer to happen than you think they will, and then they happen faster than you thought they could."

Rudiger Dornbusch

In general, the impact of higher commodity prices on a particular economy depends on whether that economy is a net exporter or importer of commodities. For many developed economies, which tend to be net importers of commodities, higher commodity prices generally act like a tax, by making it more expensive to import the materials and energy required for their economies to function. In contrast, economies that are net exporters of commodities tend to benefit from higher prices because they earn more revenue from the sale of those commodities; this is only up to a point though, because if prices increase by too much and too fast, then this may reduce the demand for commodities by industrialised countries.

The price of oil is particularly important given its dominance in power generation, transport and industry. In the 1970s, OPEC member states restricted oil production, resulting in a sharp increase in the price of oil. Since oil and its derivatives are so important to industrialised economies, a large and sharp increase in its price will probably lead to higher prices for most products, raising overall inflation (known as cost push inflation) and reducing productivity (see Chapter 34 for more discussion about commodity markets and their vulnerability to cartels).

The consequences for global economic activity from a change in the price of oil will also depend on its cause. If the price of oil is driven higher by an increase in the demand for oil, then the global economy is likely to continue to expand, and perhaps at a fast pace. However, that does not rule out the possibility of recessions in individual economies, particularly if the increase in the demand for oil is concentrated in a particular country or region. On the contrary, an increase in the price of oil that is driven by a reduction in oil supply will unequivocally lower productive potential around the world, and perhaps by enough to cause the global economy to contract.[59]

Since the 1970s, almost every spike in the price of oil has been followed, relatively rapidly, by a recession in the Western world. An oil price danger zone if you like. Writing in 2005, US economist James Hamilton found that a spike in oil prices had preceded nine out of ten post-World War II US recessions. He later concluded that the economic downturn of 2007-08 should be added to the list of recessions to which oil prices appear to have made a material contribution.[60]

The demand for oil tends to be very price inelastic in the short term, meaning that end users take time to change their consumption habits in the event of a price spike (eg, buy a more energy efficient car or start using public transport). Consumers and businesses cannot react quickly enough to a sudden spike in commodity prices to protect their ability to spend, acting as a brake on economic growth (see Chapter 22 on commodity volatility). In contrast, gradual increases in commodity prices and oil, in particular, tend not to be so damaging to economic growth; businesses and consumers are able to adjust more smoothly. Moreover, it can take time for changes in underlying virgin commodity prices to be reflected in the prices for goods that you and I pay in the shops. For example, businesses may have hedged their exposure to commodity prices (see Chapter 31 on managing risk in commodity markets).[61] Over time, however, there is more opportunity to react to high prices or the threat of a disruption to supply. Businesses and governments may start looking at investing in reduced energy and resource intensive means of production, or looking for alternative sources of supply or indeed other commodities that can act as a substitute.[62]

Remember to bear in mind that different sectors of the economy are exposed to different commodity prices. For example, airlines and car manufacturers may be adversely affected by a rise in the cost of oil, while oil services companies benefit. At the same time, food and drink manufacturers facing higher oil and agricultural prices will have to endure higher operating and input costs.

So far we have looked at the impact on economic growth from the negative point of view that higher prices are bad. What about a positive shock to commodity prices? This question has been especially relevant for the US since 2008/09 when gas prices have plummeted because of rising shale gas output, spurring investment by energy intensive manufacturers like petrochemicals etc. Previous studies have concluded that sharp price reductions tend not to have much of a stimulative effect on economic growth in the US and other industrialised economies, meaning that an economy tends to respond asymmetrically to changes in oil prices. However, again, the reason for the sharp fall in prices (whether it is demand or supply led) may have a bearing on its impact on economic growth.[63]

The picture for any one country is further complicated if they are a large producer, as well as being a large consumer of a commodity. For the US, the sharp drop in the price of oil from mid-2014 was a boost to consumers, but it also resulted in job losses in the energy industry. Given the significant investment that took place in the country's shale extraction industry, lower oil prices meant that banks, financial institutions and other investors were also exposed to potential losses, further muddying the waters.

Don't forget the exchange rate when checking to see the impact of commodity prices on an economy. Just because a commodity is priced in dollar terms doesn't mean you shouldn't view the market in Euro, sterling or any other currency, because the picture may be very different. For example, high commodity prices may be a burden for one country, but a disaster for another whose currency has depreciated sharply against the dollar and is heavily dependent on the import of foreign oil.

Commodity prices, freight costs and other indicators are often pointed to as potential gauges of underlying economic activity. However, just looking at the price of a commodity and the cost of transporting it tells you nothing about whether higher prices indicate a strengthening in demand or a cut in supply (see Chapter 12 and Chapter 32 for more on Doctor Copper and the Baltic Dry Index).

The essential thing:

A sharp increase in commodity prices can act as a tax on countries that are dependent on the consumption of commodities, putting a brake on economic growth.

20) China

"There is simply no overstating China's importance to all of us, not just to 1.3 billion Chinese. The entire planet, all 6.5 billion of us, is invested in China's success."

Jim O'Neil

At different points in history, the growth of economies from Britain to Japan resulted in these countries becoming the hub for commodity markets, pulling in resources from around the globe. Over the past 200-plus years, there have been several major swings in commodity prices. The longest, broadest and most sustained upswings are spawned when there is a new source of demand. The upswing from 1815 to 1855 was sparked by the Industrial Revolution in Britain and the migration to the cities it engendered. Then, from 1875 to 1914, Germany, and then the US, experienced the industrialisation and urbanisation pattern. The cycle from the mid-1950s to the 1990s occurred when Japan, Korea, Taiwan and others all followed, in quick succession, a similar industrialisation-begets-urbanisation blueprint.

During the recent commodity price upswing, China has been the single biggest driver of commodity demand. This reflects both industrialisation – China has become the world's factory – and urbanisation – China has needed significant quantities of commodities to meet its infrastructure requirements as more people move to cities and demand housing, commercial buildings and transportation.[64]

Between 1994 and 2014, China went from consuming 8% of the global aluminium supply to 51% in 2014. A very similar pattern emerges across other commodities: China's share of global consumption for nickel increased from 5% to 51%; zinc from 11% to 45% and copper from 8% to 45%. In contrast, China's share in the global consumption of oil has only risen from 5% in 1994 to just 12% in 2014.[65]

The extent to which China's demand for commodities would rise in the early 2000s was largely unanticipated by commodity producers, leading to a long period of underinvestment. This partly reflects that China's industrialisation was more rapid than other Asian economies, reflecting China's preference for industrial-led development.

As explained elsewhere in this book, a number of commodities are in the hands of one or a few large sellers, which may allow them to use their market power to extract higher prices for the commodities. On the other side is the monopsonist, a large buyer that can dictate terms to suppliers. China has frequently been described as a monopsonist, buying significant proportions of global commodity supplies.

Chinese demand for commodities, more so than other emerging economies, is driven by the policies put in place by its leaders – policies that have sought to cover a wide range of strategic objectives. Security of supply is particularly important, ensuring that its citizens have enough food in the event of a natural disaster. China has built up vast reserves of agricultural commodities like wheat and corn, and it is often estimated that China has stored enough to cover consumption for its citizens for a whole year.[66]

In the spirit of a monopsonist, Chinese companies have actively purchased land and mineral rights across the globe for a range of different commodities.[67] In mid-2007, a Chinese company, Chinalco, bought the mineral rights to mine the resources contained in Mount Toromocho in Peru for $3 billion. The mountain, more than half the height of Mount Everest, is estimated to contain two billion tonnes of copper, one of the largest single copper deposits in the world.

Despite China's undoubted influence on global commodity markets, developments in its economy continue to remain opaque and hence so too are its implications for commodity prices. Li Keqiang – now Chinese premier, but previously known as the head of Liaoning province's communist party – admitted over dinner with the US ambassador to China in 2007 that the country's GDP figures were "man-made" and therefore unreliable. Mr Li went on to say that instead he concentrated on just three data points – electricity consumption, rail cargo volume and bank lending – when evaluating his province's economic progress. Unfortunately for him, Wikileaks made sure that details of this conversation got around a bit.[68]

Relying on too narrow an indicator can be misleading, however. During 2007, the economy of the Liaoning province was largely driven by heavy industry, and so it was very reasonable for Li Keqiang to look at these data. However, Liaoning was and is still more reliant on heavy industry than the rest of the country, and the structure of the national economy has changed dramatically since 2007, with services now accounting for a larger share of the economy than industry.[69]

As China's economy continues to develop, the composition of commodities it consumes will probably continue to evolve. Richer Chinese consumers are stoking demand for dairy products, meat, chocolate, jewellery etc. That has an effect both on those items directly and on the commodities used to produce them. Although imports of iron ore wane, for example, as infrastructure spending slows; demand for soybeans, which are used mainly to feed livestock, has accelerated.

Commodities are also used in China as collateral or security for a loan for cash strapped companies unable to secure credit using traditional banking channels. Commodities used as collateral tend to have a high value-to-density ratio, such as gold, silver or nickel (note that despite being bulkier and perishable, agricultural commodities like soybeans and natural rubber are increasingly playing a similar role). Various estimates suggest that approximately one-third of copper imported into China may have been passing through financing deals.[70]

China's impact on commodity markets is starting to evolve in other ways too. As the world's biggest importer of commodities, it makes sense for China to be able to control the means by which prices are formed. Up until now China has had to rely on commodity price benchmarks, like Brent for oil, which are often based on physical fundamentals on the other side of the globe (see Chapter 43 on how commodity prices are discovered). Now, in an attempt to ensure that commodities are traded the way it wants, China is starting to introduce its own commodity futures contracts, centred on significant Chinese importing regions and denominated in yuan rather than US dollars.

The essential thing:

China has been the single biggest driver of global commodity demand since the late 1990s.

21) The resource curse

"When a nation is over-reliant on one or two commodities like oil or precious minerals, corrupt government ministers and their dodgy associates hoard profits and taxes instead of properly allocating them to schools and hospitals."

Bono

In the early 16th century, the Spanish conquistador Francisco Pizarro ended the Inca Empire, killing Emperor Atahualpa. After looting immense hoards of gold, silver and other treasures, and then destroying the Incan capital Cusco, Pizarro founded Lima, the present day capital of Peru. So far so brutal, but did the riches prove to be a blessing or a curse?

Not many countries are named after commodities. There is Argentina, from the Latin word for silver. Panama and Uruguay are thought to be indigenous words for fish. Brazil became known for its Brazil wood, the source of a valuable dye. Finally, of course, ivory from the Ivory Coast. However, discovering that your nation has a bounty of commodities may not be as good as it sounds.[71]

The resource curse typically describes the apparent relationship between the increase in a country's exploitation of natural resources and a decline in the manufacturing or agricultural sector of the economy. The relationship is also known as the Dutch disease. A term first coined in 1977 by The Economist magazine to describe the decline of the manufacturing sector in the Netherlands after the discovery of a large natural gas field in 1959.[72]

A resource boom affects an economy in two significant ways. First, in the "resource movement effect", the resource boom will increase the demand for labour, causing production to shift toward the booming sector and away from the manufacturing and agricultural sectors. However, this effect may be negligible because the energy and mineral extraction sectors generally employ very few people. The second and more significant impact is known as the "spending effect". This occurs as a result of the extra revenue brought in by the resource boom, increasing the demand for labour in the service sector and shifting labour away from manufacturing. This shift is also known as indirect-deindustrialisation.

A guy who works at a furniture factory, for example, might see that mowing the lawn of the nearby mansion is more lucrative and change professions. But that movement of labour also means, on a broader scale, that the country stops producing some of the goods it used to produce. The impact is made worse because commodity exports may help to drive up the value of the currency, making other parts of the economy less competitive and adversely affecting the current-account balance. The furniture factory is therefore no longer as profitable, is no longer able to export its products competitively and instead the country starts to import furniture.[73]

Resource exploitation can also have an impact on inequality within a country because those few people who own mines or oil wells will profit when prices rise. For oil exploration and production, relatively few people from the host country are employed because operators often prefer to bring in more experienced personnel from overseas. This concentration of wealth only serves to perpetuate indirect-deindustrialisation, leading to higher imports of luxury goods and higher demand for luxury services.

An abundance of natural resource wealth can also distort economies in a number of other ways. Private investment in other less exploitable/profitable sectors of the economy may stagnate, leaving the government and economy highly dependent on resource revenues. This may be okay when commodity prices are high, but if they decline or suffer high volatility, and the economy is reliant on one commodity, then the economy becomes very vulnerable. Moreover, what if available supplies of oil, mineral or other commodity run out? As we saw, a commodity boom may hollow out the manufacturing sector. If the commodity boom turns to bust, the country has nothing to fall back on.

A further problem is the potentially corrosive effect of commodity production on political institutions. Many commodities incorporate rents (ie, excess profits derived from the fact that supply is usually limited in the short term). Given that many commodity producers are owned and managed by the government, it is in the state's interest to capture those rents, but corruption often follows when it does.

Over-reliance on the production of commodities may also fuel civil war. Research by Oxford University found that for any given five year period, the chance of a civil war in an African country varies from less than 1% in countries without resource wealth to nearly 25% in those with such riches. Clearly, countries that are afflicted by civil unrest are also less likely to be able to grow their economies and develop and maintain democratic institutions.[74]

The Prebisch-Singer hypothesis suggests that the prices of mineral and agricultural products follow a downward trajectory in the long run, relative to the prices of manufactured goods and other products. As we saw in Chapter 7, the long run real rate of return on commodities tends towards zero. Concentrating on the production and export of one or a few commodities means that a country's income, which although might benefit in the short term from a commodities boom, may suffer in the long term.

Related to this is commodity volatility (see more on the causes and costs of volatility in Chapter 22), if an economy is overly exposed to fluctuations in one commodity then this imposes economic costs. For example, cyclical shifts of resources (labour and land) back and forth across sectors – mineral, agricultural, manufacturing and services – may incur needless transaction costs.

Back to the story of Pizarro and the silver…

After the conquests of South America by the Spanish Empire, silver from the mines in South America were shipped back to Spain to finance wars in Europe. The convoys of ships – up to a hundred at a time – transported 170 tons of silver across the Atlantic a year. However, the Spanish monarchs of the 16th century, Charles V and Philips II, found that an abundance of precious metal could be as much a curse as a blessing. The reason? They dug up so much silver to pay for their wars of conquest, that the metal itself dramatically declined in value.[75]

The essential thing:

Resources can be a curse as well as a blessing.

Want to know more? Visit my blog **Materials Risk** *and get email updates and analysis on what's really happening in commodities and commodity markets.*

22) Commodity volatility

"What commodity prices lack in trend, they make up for in variance."

Angus Deaton

A crucial distinction when talking about commodity price volatility is that of variability and unpredictability. Prices exhibit variability for many reasons, but some price changes may be more predictable than others. For example, agricultural prices tend to be lowest during and soon after harvest, and highest immediately before harvest. Although seasonal changes are not exactly constant from year to year, they are often similar from one year to the next. Weather shocks, on the other hand, are typically unpredictable. Adverse weather conditions may lead to unpredictable changes in prices, especially if stocks are low to begin with.[76]

Commodity prices tend to be more volatile than many other prices in the economy because, in the short term, both supply and demand are relatively price inelastic. Increasing commodity production takes time if new crops must be grown, mineral exploration undertaken or oil wells drilled. Similarly, it can take considerable time to change consumption habits, such as shifting from coal-fired electricity generation to gas or altering the share of more fuel-efficient cars. This sluggish response means that supply and demand shocks, whether it is an adverse weather event or a natural disaster, can result in large price movements. If demand grows faster than supply, then stock levels will run down, perhaps alongside higher commodity prices. The absence of a buffer means that in turn the market may now be more vulnerable to a further shock to demand or supply. Note that this does not mean that high prices are by necessity always correlated with high volatility.

In commodities, inventories may be measured in terms of "weeks' consumption" – an estimate of the number of weeks of consumption that existing inventories can last. When inventories fall below a certain number of weeks, it breaches a psychological barrier in which people get nervous, and coupled with a strong transient shock (such as a strike at a mine or a crop failure affecting a particular season's produce), this uncertainty may cause price volatility to increase.

Commodity price volatility is closely related to the ability to store the commodity. In the most extreme example in which the commodity cannot be stored for immediate delivery, such as electricity, prices are the most volatile. In terms of natural gas and oil, which can be stored but require specialised infrastructure, volatility is low when inventories are available, but spikes occur when infrastructure constraints are approached.

Metals and agriculture stand in sharp contrast to energy because they do not run into storage capacity constraints as quickly. For metals, all one needs is a parking lot and a chain link fence and you can stack the metals as high as you want. As a result, the volatility of non-energy commodities is generally lower and only spikes when inventories approach depletion.

The steepness of the commodity cost curve can also influence the volatility of a commodity. As we saw in Chapter 4, the commodity cost curve tends to influence commodity prices over the longer term. Different commodities have different shaped commodity cost curves depending on their underlying production characteristics. For example, iron ore has a particularly steep curve at the high end of the cost curve. In this example, so long as prices are relatively high and the whole cost curve is in play, iron ore prices are very sensitive to shifts in the supply/demand balance and so are subject to high volatility. As demand falls, the market quickly becomes less reliant on the higher cost producers and therefore the commodity price drops sharply because these producers are no longer required to satisfy demand.[77]

High commodity price volatility tends to hurt producers the most, especially farmers who make all their investments in seeds, fertiliser and equipment at the start of the growing season, before the post-harvest price is known. If prices in the year ahead look unstable, farmers may invest less than usual, with the consequence that they no longer maximise profits and also produce less food to sell.

Commodity price volatility also presents a cost to the consumer of those commodities too. Thinking about a manufacturer of an essential widget for the iPhone, a significant change in the price of a significant input can negatively affect the economics of manufacturing and the commercial viability of the end product. Uncertainty over the cost structure of a business can deter investment because businesses are less able to budget for the future (see Chapter 31 for how businesses can respond).

Commodity price volatility can also have implications for whole economies. Many commodity producing countries are significantly dependent on the production and the export of a handful of commodities. The performance of their overall economy, government revenues and hence the amount they have to spend on things like health and education will fluctuate with commodity prices (see Chapter 23 on how adding value can help economies act as a buffer to underlying commodity prices).

At first sight, unstable food prices are likely to have a greater detrimental effect on consumers in low income countries. Here, food accounts for a large share of consumer spending, although people tend to have less access to banking facilities to be able to cope with the volatility. However, since different food staples are often substitutable, commodity price volatility may not be quite as damaging for consumers. For instance, changes in the price of one commodity are not perfectly correlated with changes in the price of another, so consumers may be able to adjust their purchases to take advantage of relative discounts.[78]

Economies dependent on commodities for manufacturing and supporting service industries may also be exposed to commodity price volatility. As global supply chains become increasingly entwined and have moved towards "just in time delivery", this has meant that volatility in primary commodities is likely to be transmitted through supply chains to the end consumer much faster than ever before.

The essential thing:

Commodity prices are inherently volatile, creating uncertainty for business, deterring investment and/or leading to less than optimal decisions.

23) Comparative advantage

"If a foreign country can supply us with a commodity cheaper than we ourselves can make it, better buy it of them with some part of the produce of our own industry, employed in a way in which we have some advantage."

Adam Smith

Consider Finland, a Nordic country endowed with many trees for its small population. A classical economist would argue that given this, the country should export wood. By contrast, a traditional development economist would argue that it should add value by transforming the wood into paper or furniture. But for Finland, wood opened up a different and even richer path to development. As the Finns were chopping wood, their axes and saws would become dull and break down and they would have to be repaired or replaced. This eventually led them to become good at producing machines that chop and cut wood. These machines eventually led to Nokia.[79]

In economics, the theory of comparative advantage refers to the ability of an individual, business or country to produce a particular good or service at a lower marginal and opportunity cost than another. For commodity producing countries this theory is often used to suggest that if, like the Ivory Coast, you have an advantage in producing cocoa, you should do exactly that and leave the business of turning it into chocolate to someone else. However, an economy that is too dependent on one or few commodities can be a problem. The resource curse, as it's known, can result in other sectors of the economy being crowded out, corruption as revenues from commodity sales are poorly managed, increased risk of armed conflict and can be costly in terms of exposure to volatile commodity prices (see more in Chapter 22).

One of the significant arguments against the approach suggested by comparative advantage is known as the Prebisch-Singer hypothesis. What this means is that countries that export primary goods and do not have the means to manufacture goods to export, will lose out in the long run because their goods will become relatively cheaper than the manufactured ones. A common explanation for this is the observation that the income elasticity of demand for manufactured goods is greater than that for virgin commodities – especially food. As incomes rise, the demand for manufactured goods increases more rapidly than the demand for virgin commodities.

In three-quarters of African economies, the share of primary commodities in total exports is 50% or more. In one-third of the continent's economies, that share rises to at least 90%. Concentration doesn't just exist by sector, but by commodity too. In eight African countries, one single commodity accounts for more than 70% of exports. Many, though, rely on a combination of agriculture, mining and energy. However, the level of value-add is very low in Africa. For example, the world's top three cocoa exporters (Ivory Coast, Ghana and Nigeria) have a very low level of value added, typically 10-20%.[80] The first and primary benefit of moving up the value chain is to capture a greater proportion of income from the value chain. However, this requires competitive processing industries and access to marketing and distribution networks.

The diamond industry provides a useful example of the current situation. Although some value accrues at the extraction stage, the retail value of processed jewels is more than three times the value of the rough stone. Yet most African producers have traditionally been excluded from any value-adding, forward-processing links, including sorting, valuing and grading.

Even if you've got an oil well on your property in West Texas, you'll still drive to the gas station to buy refined gasoline for your pickup truck; you may grow wheat on a family farm but odds are that you're still buying flour for bread (if not ready-made bread) in a store. So even though a country like Iran produces a lot of oil, it still needs to import gasoline to fuel its cars.[81]

Most products require many inputs and, often, one raw material will just not make a large enough difference. For example, Australia, despite its remoteness, is a major exporter of iron ore, but not of steel; whereas South Korea is an exporter of steel, but must import iron ore.[82]

The moral of the story is that adding value to raw materials is one path to diversification. However, countries are not limited by the raw materials they have. After all, Switzerland has no cocoa.

The essential thing:

Many countries that are dependent on the sale of one or a few commodities may look to add value to those commodities in order to increase their economic development.

24) The "Fifth Fuel" and the Jevons Paradox

"It is wholly a confusion of ideas to suppose that the economical use of fuel is equivalent to a diminished consumption. The very contrary is the truth."

William Stanley Jevons

Energy efficiency, sometimes called conservation, is also known as the "fifth fuel" (after coal, petroleum, nuclear power and renewables). Improvements in energy efficiency in 11 International Energy Agency (IEA) member countries since the 1970s have saved the equivalent of 1.4 billion tonnes of oil in 2011, worth $743 billion.[83] This saving amounted to more than their total final consumption of gas, coal or any other single fuel in that year. And lots of money is being invested in doing even better; an estimated $310-$360 billion was spent on energy efficiency measures worldwide in 2012, more than what was invested in either renewables or in fossil fuel generation.[84]

The basic challenge to energy efficiency is the same around the world. Energy efficiency is not one big thing; it is embodied in everything – buildings that operate more cleverly, cars that get more miles to the gallon, factories that put in new technologies and reduce energy use in manufacturing goods and planes that get better mileage in the skies. So how can the pace of improvement in energy efficiency be stepped up? There is no single answer but price certainly counts. In response to high jet fuel costs, airlines have been doing everything they can to reduce fuel use – from changing descent paths to getting rid of magazines in order to reduce weight. All industries, for which energy costs are a big cost item, are similarly motivated. Rising gasoline prices have helped change the minds of consumers and car manufacturers alike.[85]

Regulations help to reinforce energy efficiency. The latest fuel efficiency standards require new designs and new technologies and weight reduction. In the building sector, new construction codes promote designs that are more efficient; but the impact in that sector takes time, both for know-how to spread throughout the industry and because the stock of buildings turns over so slowly. Remember, buildings tend to account for the largest single chunk of final energy consumption.

But is energy efficiency as good as it first appears? Could greater energy efficiency actually be offset by higher energy consumption? The question first had its origins at the start of the Industrial Revolution, and became known as the Jevons

Paradox. In 1865, the book "The Coal Question" was published, arguing that the UK's economic prosperity was at risk because the country would run out of reserves of coal, and rebutting critics who suggested that as steam engines became more efficient, demand for coal would fall or at least not rise as fast. The author, William Stanley Jevons, offered the example of the British iron industry. If some technological advance made it possible for a blast furnace to produce iron with less coal, then profits would rise, new investment in iron production would be attracted and the price of iron would fall, thereby stimulating additional demand. Eventually he concluded, "The greater number of furnaces will more than make up for the diminished consumption of each."[86]

Jevons argued that energy efficiency does not reduce energy consumption. You only have to look around you for examples of why Jevons might be right. When light was hugely expensive, a person might read by the flame of a single candle; now, light is so cheap (relative to total spending in the whole economy at least) that we flood our cities with it.[87]

In a paper published in 1998, the Yale economist William D. Nordhaus estimated the cost of lighting throughout human history. An ancient Babylonian, he calculated, needed to work more than 41 hours to acquire enough lamp oil to provide 1,000 lumen-hours of light – the equivalent of a 75 watt incandescent bulb burning for approximately an hour. Three and a half thousand years later, a contemporary of Thomas Jefferson's could buy the same amount

128

of illumination, in the form of tallow candles, by working for approximately five hours and twenty minutes. By 1992, an average American, with access to compact fluorescents, could do the same in less than half a second.[88]

What happens to all those energy savings that consumers and businesses make? In addition to the effect outlined by Jevons, the rebound effect, as it is known, suggests that consumers will spend and invest those savings on other products and services. If everyone reacts that way then this will lead, indirectly, to an increase in demand for energy and other commodities.

Even here you really have to look at the really big macro picture, the globe, to see it in action. For example, in the UK, energy consumption per person is at its lowest level for 50 years, yet global energy consumption continues to increase despite a cornucopia of efficiency gains over the decades.

The essential thing:

Efficiency gains may reduce energy and resource consumption in the short term, but in supporting economic growth this may create new demands for commodities, potentially swamping the initial saving.

*Congratulations, you're almost halfway through the book. Want to know more? Visit my blog **Materials Risk** and get email updates and analysis on what's really happening in commodities and commodity markets.*

25) Malthus

"Yet in all societies, even those that are most vicious, the tendency to a virtuous attachment is so strong that there is a constant effort towards an increase of population. This constant effort as constantly tends to subject the lower classes of the society to distress and to prevent any great permanent amelioration of their condition."

Thomas Malthus

Fear of food scarcity is a recurring theme throughout history, with the next doomsayer always willing to predict catastrophe. Thomas Robert Malthus was a British cleric and scholar. His principle work "An Essay on the Principle of Population", published in 1798, suggested that although population rises exponentially, agricultural output could only increase arithmetically because of the finite amount of land available.[89] As a result, "positive checks" (described by Malthus as higher mortality caused by famine, disease and war) were necessary to bring the number of people back in line with the capacity to feed them. How very depressing!

In the second edition, published in 1803, Malthus softened his original harsh message by introducing the idea of moral restraint. Such a "preventive check", operating through the birth rather than the death rate, could provide a way to counter the otherwise inexorable logic of too many mouths chasing too little food. If couples had fewer children, the population growth could be sufficiently slowed for agriculture to cope.

The basic tenets of Malthus' theory has, until now at least, proven to be false, because what he didn't really count on was human ingenuity. Since the 1800s, dramatic improvements in agricultural productivity, the expansion of international trade and legislative reform have resulted in vast increases in food production and lower prices. In turn, this has enabled a much larger population to be supported.[90]

The writings of Malthus are by no means the last time that concerns about population growth and the ability of the planet to cope have been voiced, and probably won't be the last. Like Malthus before him, Paul Ehrlich (ecologist, doomsayer and author of the 1968 book "THE POPULATION BOMB") believed that overpopulation would cause disaster and widespread scarcity – billions would die, developed countries would disintegrate, India was beyond saving etc. Does that sound familiar to you?

The economist Julian Simon, meanwhile, thought that people would find substitutes for scarce resources and that everything would turn out fine. To resolve their dispute the two men agreed to have a bet on the price of commodities. Ehrlich bet that the price of five metals would rise between 1980 and 1990 as scarcity gradually started to bite. Instead, metal prices fell dramatically and Ehrlich lost the bet.

More recently, the book "The Limits to Growth", commissioned by The Club of Rome, was published in 1972. In a similar vein to Malthus, the book stated that if the world's consumption patterns and population growth continued at the high rates of the time, then the earth would hit its limit within a century.

What later became known as the Malthusian Catastrophe continues to be popular to this day. The recent food price hikes of 2008-2011 have reinvigorated proponents of Malthus' theories, that the world is facing a much more difficult future that may check population growth. The ideas put forward by Malthus have since been adapted for other commodities, including energy (see more on peak oil in Chapter 26).

Environmental degradation of agricultural producing regions (lack of water, pollution etc.) may represent one of the greatest threats to the continued growth in agricultural productivity and the ability to feed a growing and increasingly wealthy human population (see Chapter 41 on commodities and sustainability). However, agricultural productivity may well continue to rise as investments in farm equipment, genetically modified food and improvements in the way food is handled from farm to plate boost food availability (see Chapter 35 on technology and innovation).

The essential thing:

Malthus thought that since agricultural output could only increase arithmetically, whereas population would continue to rise exponentially, sooner or later population growth would be checked by famine and disease.

26) Peak oil and resource scarcity

"Understanding depletion is simple. Think of an Irish pub. The glass starts full and ends empty. There are only so many more drinks to closing time. It's the same with oil. We have to find the bar before we can drink what is in it."

Colin Campbell

"Long queues formed at the stations with petrol – and anyone who tried to sneak ahead in the queue met raw violence…."[91] No, this isn't some description of a dystopic future. It actually happened in the early 1970s, when Arab oil producing nations convulsed most of the world by tightening the spigots on their wells, sharply reducing oil production and sending the price of oil soaring. The impact it had on people's lives in Australia provided the inspiration for the film *Mad Max*. Building on the experiences of the 1970s, and tapping into fears that oil was going to run out, the film describes a dystopic future Australia where law and order has begun to break down following a major energy crisis. In the film, most of the Australian Outback has been reduced to low-populated communities with low fuel supplies but a relatively peaceful life, with major metropolitan cities continuing to exist. However, motorcycle gangs scavenge the lands and terrorise the population.

Mad Max wasn't the first time fears over our future energy needs were identified, but it was the first time it was brought to popular attention (at least implicitly albeit very violently in the film). For it was back in 1956 that M. King Hubbert predicted that US oil and gas production would peak in the 1970s and then decline. The famous forecast of peaking oil and gas production came to be known as "Hubbert's peak" and spawned the popular and influential theory known as "peak oil".

The peak oil theory is based on the observation that the amount of oil under the ground in any region is finite and so the rate of discovery, which at first increases quickly, must eventually reach a maximum and decline. The term "peak oil" refers to a hypothetical date after which oil production will gradually diminish, with oil production following a bell curve, leading to permanent upward pressure on oil prices.

The idea started to gain enormous popularity in the early 1970s when US oil output peaked. At the time, the US and other oil dependent nations were groaning under the weight of high prices and long queues for gasoline after OPEC restricted output. Meanwhile, other forecasters like Paul Ehrlich became celebrities, with dire warnings of overpopulation and the exhaustion of natural resources (see Chapter 25 on Malthus and other dire warnings).

Hubbert was a geologist, not an economist. The peak oil theory was based on the assumption that both technology and prices are fixed. This means that the amount of reserves that are currently economical to produce will go on to be produced until the reserve runs out.

Other geologists have come forward since Hubbert's time, making similar predictions. Colin Campbell, a retired British geologist who worked for major oil companies between 1957 and 1990, predicted that global oil production would peak around 2005. Others have made similar predictions of world output peaking somewhere between 2005 and 2015.

By far the most outspoken Cassandra in the oil business has been Matthew Simmons. Simmons has published research questioning the validity of the Saudi's reserve estimates, arguing that all of the kingdoms giant oil fields have already peaked and that the easy flows of the past are gone.[92]

Are we running out of oil and indeed other commodities? Resources on Earth are certainly finite, but that does not mean that they are genuinely scarce. The reserves of oil and other commodities that Hubbert and others refer to is the supply of commodities that can be extracted economically with current technology. The basic concept behind the peak oil theory is applicable to metals and minerals, as well as other energy sources like gas and coal. However, even in one of the more contentiously rare metals, copper, there is little evidence to support the thesis that commodities are becoming genuinely scarce. Indeed, reserve/production ratios have fluctuated between 30 and 60 years for the past 80 years. Even focusing on the most recent super-cycle period of rising copper prices, 178 million tonnes of copper were mined during the period 2004-2014. Over the same period, copper reserves grew by 230 million tonnes.[93] [94]

In reality, a commodity shortage leads to higher prices and in turn incentivises the development of improved technology that may ultimately lead to the discovery and exploitation of more reserves, perhaps those that were previously uneconomic. Using an extreme scenario, suppose you told me that as a result of a careful examination of oil reservoirs, you were certain that annual oil production was just about to plummet and would be 30% below its current level in two years. Under this scenario oil is going to become extremely valuable in a short period of time. Anybody who pumps a barrel out of a reservoir today to sell at the current price could make many multiple times as much money if they just left it in the ground another two years before pumping it out. If oil producers respond to these very strong incentives by holding back oil from today's market, the effect would be to drive today's price up. What impact would that have?[95]

For one thing, it would be a very powerful and effective incentive to force today's users of oil to reduce their consumption immediately. It would also be a very powerful incentive for investing heavily in alternative oil extraction technologies and other sources of energy. And, of course, it would leave us more oil in the future to keep the economy going as we make the required transitions. In other words, the consequence of oil producers trying to sell their oil for the highest price would be to help move society immediately and powerfully in the direction that we earlier determined it ought to move in anticipation of what is going to happen in the future.

Indeed this was how it has turned out. Hubbert's predictions proved premature because the development of new production techniques made the exploitation of previously uneconomic areas commercially viable (see Chapter 35 for more discussion on commodity prices, innovation and investment). Indeed, the advent of the shale era in the US brings this into stark focus.

A bunch of leather-clad bikers dishing out violence might make for great entertainment, but it is not necessarily what the future holds. Our ability to adapt to the changing world around us and to stop the world from degenerating is frequently underestimated.

The essential thing:

The peak oil theory suggests that oil production will peak and go into terminal decline, leading to permanent upward pressure on oil prices.

27) Resource nationalism

"If there was any armed aggression against Venezuela from Colombian territory or from anywhere else, promoted by the Yankee empire, we would suspend oil shipments to the United States, even if we have to eat stones here."

Hugo Chavez, former Venezuelan President

Resource nationalism describes a government's effort to gain greater control or value from its natural resources. This can range from outright expropriation – when a government takes away a private company's assets – to more creeping forms of appropriation – such as higher taxation or tougher regulation. Although resource nationalism may be driven by economic interest, improving bilateral relations, diplomatic ambitions and popular sentiment also play a role in nationalism policies.[96]

In 1938, the Mexican oil industry was nationalised. Seen in the context of its people, it was viewed that, at last, a poor country, long buffeted by predatory foreign powers, had exercised its right to own the wealth of its subsoil, seeing off rich countries that treated access to these resources at low cost as their right. Meanwhile, in 1951, the Iranian government nationalised the assets of the Anglo-Iranian Oil Company (now known as BP). The decision was enormously popular within the country and seen as a long overdue staunching of its national wealth that could now be harnessed to fighting poverty in Iran. More recently, in Venezuela, the late Hugo Chávez grasped strategic assets to propagate his Bolivarian revolution. Bolivia and Ecuador followed his cue.

Resource nationalism may also result in higher and more volatile commodity prices. Higher political risks associated with conflicts of this sort will also compound uncertainty in global resource markets. Should fear of expropriation or resource nationalism keep investors away from attractive deposits and deter future investments, it could result in global supply constraints and higher commodity price volatility.

Although a government may appear to be good, transparent and welcoming to foreign producers, years later – once a mine or an oil well has opened – they may change their tune. This time inconsistency and resulting uncertainty may reduce longer term investment in the country's resource productivity; leading to a loss of skills and capital from the private sector, reducing production and potentially leading to higher volatility.

A recent example of this process in action is Venezuela, where in 2003 Hugo Chávez, the president at the time, fired more than 18,000 employees of the state-run oil corporation, Petróleos de Venezuela (PDVSA), and banned them from working for any company doing business with PDVSA. At the stroke of a pen, the oil company lost approximately half of its managers and technicians. Despite the strong rise in oil prices since 2003, the loss of so many experienced workers was one reason why the country has failed to benefit and oil production in Venezuela has stagnated.[97]

Countries such as Russia and Ukraine introduced export bans on agricultural commodities during the period 2008–12, a decision designed to protect domestic consumers from higher food prices. However, these export restrictions may have exacerbated concerns about global agricultural supplies and in turn contributed to higher global food prices.

Restrictions on agricultural commodity exports are legal under global commerce rules, even for those countries (such as Ukraine) that are bound by their membership to the World Trade Organisation (WTO). *The General Agreement on Tariffs and Trade*, the core treaty of the WTO, has banned "prohibitions or restrictions" on exports of commodities since 1947. However, it permits them when "temporarily applied to prevent or relieve critical shortages of foodstuffs or other products essential" to the exporting country. The treaty also fails to explain what it means by "temporarily" or what a "critical shortage" is, leaving countries ample room for manoeuvre.

What are the causes of resource nationalism? High commodity prices have been a significant driver of resource nationalism in the past, with foreign multinationals often accused of pocketing excessive windfalls or not doing enough to extract a valuable and scarce resource. However, as the shale revolution has taken hold in the US and the perceptions of the relative scarcity of oil and other commodities have changed, there are tentative signs that this may have reduced the ability of the governments of commodity producing countries to negotiate (or impose) better terms on international resource companies.

A decline in commodity prices doesn't necessarily signal the end of resource nationalism though. A slowdown in economic growth may also drive resource nationalism because governments dependent on their sale try and get a bigger share of a shrinking pie.

The essential thing:

Resource nationalism describes a government's effort to gain greater control or value from its natural resources, often at the expense of property rights.

*Want to know more? Visit my blog **Materials Risk** and get email updates and analysis on what's really happening in commodities and commodity markets.*

28) Geopolitics

"The world is exploding all over."

Chuck Hagel, US Secretary of Defence

Despite what you may hear in the news, the scramble between nations for resources does not just involve crude oil. During the American civil war in the 1860s, the South was primarily a cotton-based economy and Britain, its largest customer, was the most powerful economy in the world. Since Britain relied on American cotton to run its dominant textile industry, Jefferson Davis (President of the Confederate States during the civil war) calculated that embargoing cotton exports would help shift the British from their position of neutrality to a position of support for the Confederate cause. It was a huge miscalculation. The "cotton famine", and the resulting spike in cotton prices in the early 1860s, encouraged additional production elsewhere in the world and deprived the Confederacy of its main source of revenues.

So what exactly is geopolitics?

In 2009, political scientists Ian Bremmer and Preston Keat defined geopolitics as: "The study of how geography, politics, strategy, and history combine to generate the rise and fall of great powers and wars among states."

Given its importance to the running of the modern global economy, nowhere is this more vividly observed than in the battle for energy resources and, in particular, oil. A cursory look at a simple oil price chart dating back to the 1970s reveals a series of bumps. Each of these can be pinpointed to wars and conflicts, whether it was the Iranian revolution, the Iraqi invasion of Kuwait or the US-led invasion of Iraq. More recently, Arab Spring-related uprisings in Libya or Egypt, civil war in Syria and violence in Iraq and the Ukraine have resulted in escalating geopolitical tensions across many important energy production and transit countries.

There is a strong correlation between war casualties in energy producing countries and disruptions to oil output. After all, as many historical episodes suggest, oil development and distribution systems are hard to keep running when countries are immersed in civil wars or wars with neighbouring countries (see Chapter 41 for more discussion on conflict minerals).[98]

The expansion in oil and gas output from shale deposits in the US could change geopolitical risk in energy markets as the US becomes a net energy exporter in years to come. The impact that this shift could have on global geopolitics is uncertain. Indeed, the massive potential for developing unconventional oil and gas reserves have prompted many other countries around the world to rethink their energy policies, which will also have implications for geopolitical developments.

Even if oil prices fall, the commodity will remain geopolitically significant. Energy forms the backbone of modern industrial economies, and energy resources are critical export commodities for those who possess a lot of them. As long as fossil fuels remain the dominant source of energy, oil supply and oil prices in particular will remain critically important.

Now let's go back to the example at the start of this chapter. For a lesson on the dangers of assuming a commodity boom will last forever (see Chapter 7), as well as the impact that commodities and resources have on geopolitics, the sorry tale of Egypt's then Khedive Ismail Pasha and his hasty response to the cotton price spike is pertinent.

Officially a part of the Ottoman Empire (but highly autonomous in practice), the Egyptians had long sought formal independence. Therefore, in order to win Western support for independence, Egypt had to increase its geopolitical importance. The most obvious way to do this was to take control of the Suez Canal project that was then underway.

With the record price that cotton was now commanding on the world market, the Khedive saw his opportunity. The ambitious plan to buy out the French would be financed by borrowing against the now plentiful cotton revenues. Unfortunately, the flood of cotton revenues soon dried up. Egypt wasn't the only alternative supplier and India and Brazil were soon producing cotton too.

When the US Civil War ended, US cotton exports resumed, prices collapsed and Egypt was saddled with a debt burden it could no longer afford. The financial crisis that ultimately ensued saw the British taking over Egypt's shareholding of the canal, moving its troops in to protect its new "strategic interest" and expelling poor old Ismail the Magnificent.

More recently, rare earth elements (REEs) have taken a shot at assuming the mantle of being of great geopolitical importance. REEs have unique properties that play a crucial role in applications ranging from hybrid motors to fibre optics.[99] Until the mid-1980s, the US dominated the production of REEs, but then China moved in and by 2010 were producing over 90%. In 2010, China halted shipments of REEs to Japan, following a diplomatic crisis, and implemented export quotas, resulting in prices rising multiple times over (see Chapter 17).

Aside from the economic advantage it might bestow on China in the development of applications for REEs, as the rest of the world searches for alternatives, it also raised concerns from a geopolitical point of view, given their importance in many aerospace and defence applications and other nation's dependence on China (see Chapter 27 on resource nationalism).

Finally, climate change and the fight for resources could lead to more wars and conflict in the future. According to the Pentagon, the projected effects of climate change "...are threat multipliers that will aggravate stressors abroad such as poverty, environmental degradation, political instability social tensions – conditions that can enable terrorist activity and other forms of violence".[100]

The essential thing:

The pursuit of resources to feed growing populations and economies can lead to conflict; in turn, geopolitical conflict itself may become a risk to the supply of many commodities.

29) Strategic reserves

"...a middle course between unfettered competition under laissez-faire conditions and planned controls which try to freeze commerce into a fixed mould."

John Maynard Keynes

"...curb irresponsible movement of the price rather than establish stability within a narrow range of fluctuations."

Richard Kahn

In late 2012, news broke that thieves had stolen $18 million worth of Quebec's strategic maple syrup reserves. The Federation of Quebec Maple Syrup Producers has been managing warehouses full of surplus sweetener since 2000. The crooks made off with 60% of the province's backup supply.[101]

But why does Canada need to stockpile so much syrup? Well, harvesting maple is a fickle business. The trees need cold nights and mildly warm days to yield sap, meaning production can vary greatly, year to year, based on the weather. That's a potential problem for the big syrup buyers. If there isn't enough supply then prices could rise, potentially reducing their margins.[102]

Many governments seek to hold their own "strategic" stock of commodities aside, for emergencies, to ensure the security of supply and to counter high and volatile prices. The issue of countering the impact of large fluctuations in the price of raw materials and foods (particularly wheat) came to prominence after World War I. British economist John Maynard Keynes suggested that buffer stocks (or strategic reserves) should be built in times of peace, as well as war, to smooth commodity price fluctuations and damp down the trade cycle.[103]

The US, along with 28 other members of the International Energy Agency (IEA) – which includes Japan, Korea, Australia and most of the industrialised west – has pledged to store 90 days of oil supplies. That policy was put into place when the organisation was founded, in the aftermath of the Arab oil embargo in 1973. IEA members have also committed to work together to combat supply shortages and co-ordinate responses.

One of the most well known strategic reserves is the US' Strategic Petroleum Reserve (SPR), the largest emergency supply in the world with the capacity to hold up to 727 million barrels of oil. Most recently, it was used to offset disruptions to oil supply in the US Gulf following Hurricane Katrina in 2005 and following the political upheaval and loss of oil production in Libya in 2011. Just the threat of a release from the SPR has often been enough to temper an increase in the oil price, particularly when there has not been any actual cut to output.

China, in particular, has also sought to hold vast reserves of commodities – from cotton, to oil, to grains – in the name of security of supply. The Chinese government have been building up stocks of agricultural commodities for many years in the interests of their own food security, often citing poor logistics and environmental vulnerability. Estimates suggest that China may have built up enough stocks of grains and other foodstuffs to cover a year's consumption or more.

Pork prices are a serious matter in China, and is a significant driver of consumer inflation. Chinese consumer inflation is closely watched by authorities eager to maintain social stability and food security. For example, the "blue-ear pig" disease that forced Chinese farmers to slaughter millions of pigs in 2008 drove the country's inflation rate to its highest level in a decade.[104] To prevent further disruptions, the Chinese government established a strategic pork reserve, keeping icy warehouses around the country stocked with frozen pork for release during times of shortage. The government was forced to add to the reserve in the spring of 2010 when a glut led to prices collapsing.

Strategic reserves may also act as a floor for many commodity prices. For example, the Strategic Reserves Bureau (SRB), the Chinese government stockpile manager, has tended to purchase commodities (whether it be oil, cotton or something else) when prices are relatively weak, and the Chinese National Development and Reform Commission, in 2008, introduced a practice of raising support prices for grains, oilseeds and cotton each year to ensure good returns for farmers.

Attempts to stockpile commodities for a rainy day can have unintended consequences though. The official stockpiling system has also made price increases self-perpetuating. Warehouse managers in China held onto grain as long as possible, since they could count on the price rising every year. There was no cost to holding the grain because the government subsidised the storage costs. As a result, grain started piling up in warehouses, leaving less available in the market and creating the illusion of a shortage.[105]

Attempts to manage world commodity markets in order to achieve price objectives are not unique to the oil market or those commodities of special strategic or geopolitical interest. The 1970s, commodity price booms brought renewed interest in "managing" markets. Numerous United Nations-backed international commodity agreements were put in place, often negotiated among producing and consuming nations in order to stabilise prices at levels deemed fair to both consumers and producers. International agreements covering coffee, cocoa, sugar, tin and natural rubber were all in place during part of the final decades of the 20th century. But all of these agreements eventually collapsed, either because of their high cost or because of the way they were constructed led to the development of alternative supplies (the last agreement, covering rubber, ended when the East Asian financial crisis hit Indonesia, Malaysia and Thailand – the three significant natural rubber producing countries).[106]

The essential thing:

Governments and industries may seek to hold their own stock of commodities aside, known as strategic reserves, for emergency use, to ensure the security of supply and to help minimise price volatility.

30) Refining commodities

"Supply chains cannot tolerate even 24 hours of disruption. So if you lose your place in the supply chain because of wild behaviour you could lose a lot. It would be like pouring cement down one of your oil wells."

Thomas Freidman

Commodities are generally not in demand for their own sake, but instead they are in demand for the products that we can manufacture from them. If the only thing you could get from the grocery store were a basket of wheat, some sugar cane and coffee beans, then we would all struggle to make an edible breakfast. Similarly, if we went to fill our cars up with fuel and the only liquid coming out of the pump was crude oil then our vehicles would quickly come to a stop. For every commodity type (energy, metals and agriculture), there are a variety of different processes that are used to manufacture the products that we need and want. For example, crude oil is refined into several different products including bitumen, gasoline and kerosene; copper ore is heated to over 1,300 degrees centigrade in order to pry the copper loose from the silica, iron and sulphur; and soybeans are "crushed" to produce soy meal and soy oil.

Feedstocks are inputs in the refinery process. In the case of an oil refinery, the input is crude oil. The substances that come out at the end of the process, such as gasoline or kerosene, are known as the finished products. Commodities are extraordinarily diverse in terms of their physical characteristics. Moreover, consumers and producers often have highly idiosyncratic preferences. For instance, oil refineries are optimised to process particular types of crude oil, and different refineries are optimised differently.

Finished products have to be exactly that, finished. The products refined from commodities cannot vary from one batch to the next. Think of your car. Without standardised gasoline grades, car manufacturers would be unable to independently develop engines which maximise the use of gasoline. Similarly, certain standards of refined agricultural products might be suitable for different end markets. Imagine you are a cake manufacturer; you want to be sure that the flour you are ordering is always consistent in its quality.

Commodity refining requires huge upfront investment in capital equipment. Therefore, the refining business – whether it is producing gasoline from an oil refinery or High Density Polyethylene (HDPE) from a cracker (a type of petrochemical facility) – is typically characterised by high volumes and low margins (see Chapter 33 on commodity trading firms). This means that even small movements in the price of a refinery's commodity feedstock, whether that is crude oil, sugar, soybeans or whatever else, can have a significant impact on margins. With such high fixed costs, the owners would prefer to operate continuously, with no shutdowns. However, equipment eventually wears out and maintenance has to be regularly scheduled to avoid a prolonged shutdown. Refineries tend to plan maintenance during the periods of the year when demand is at its lowest. However, unplanned outages can occur.

Despite the fact that finished products (eg, gasoline, soybean oil etc.) are refined from a particular commodity, the price of the refined product does not necessarily follow that of the input commodity. For example, a refinery outage due to unplanned maintenance will reduce the supply of gasoline and result in an increase in gasoline prices, even if the price of crude oil – the commodity from which it was refined – has gone down. In essence, refined products are commodities in their own right (see Chapter 31 on why this knowledge is important when thinking about hedging price risk).

The main metrics you might hear on finished product demand and supply have unusual names like "crush margin", "crack spread" and "dark spread". At its most basic, these terms refer to the difference between the sales price of the refined product and the price of the feedstock. A refiner can often lock in this margin or spread, even before it has taken delivery of the feedstock, by using futures markets (for more details see Chapter 42). For example, a soybean processor can buy soybean futures (this is known as a long position), while at the same time selling soybean meal and soybean oil futures (known as a short position).

Since commodities are only in demand because of the products that we can produce from them, demand for commodities is ultimately a function of the demand for the finished products. Following the developments in downstream markets is fundamental to understanding how the demand for a particular commodity could evolve. In the case of oil refining, there are a multitude of end markets – the largest of which are transport and power generation. For example, a colder than normal winter in the US could lead to an increased demand for heating oil, thus boosting demand for crude oil. In contrast, similar weather conditions in Saudi Arabia will reduce demand for air conditioning, leading to lower crude use in the country's power generation plants.

The essential thing:

Commodities are in demand for the products that can be manufactured from them; markets for finished products react to supply and demand in the same way that commodities do.

*Want to know more? Visit my blog **Materials Risk** and get email updates and analysis on what's really happening in commodities and commodity markets.*

31) Managing commodity risk

"Risk means more things can happen than will happen."

Elroy Dimson, London Business School

"Pigs get fat, hogs get slaughtered."

Trading proverb

Prior to the introduction of futures markets in agricultural markets, a farmer was forced to sell his crop at whatever price he could get when it was ready to reap. Farmers would harvest their crop and, being at the mercy of poor transportation, try to get it to the local town to try to find a buyer. If it were a good harvest, produce would pile up, spilling out of the available storage and lie rotting on the street.

Both producers and consumers of commodities can now use derivative instruments or futures markets to hedge underlying commodity price risk. Many companies exposed to commodity price volatility though may not hedge because they feel it involves some form of gambling. They need not worry. Hedging is all about reducing the risk profile, not about making money from hedging itself. By not hedging, company managers are actually making a decision to be subject to the full force of one commodity market or another.

Hedging instruments can be arranged bilaterally or traded between physical and financial traders in commodity markets. However, given a manufacturing company's specific requirements – in terms of specification, timing and delivery (not to mention that not all commodities have functioning derivative instruments or futures markets) – this can sometimes limit the effectiveness of hedging instruments.

Futures markets are not perfect for hedging risk. Steep backwardation (see Chapter 42) may create a situation where some producers cannot hedge at a price they would like. Owing to the long time horizon that they need to bring on additional output, they may only be able to hedge at commodity prices significantly lower than nearer dated contracts.

So what else can the owners of a company that is dependent on commodities as inputs to its business do to reduce its exposure to commodity prices? In theory, companies that can pass on their commodity price risk to their customers, without having an adverse effect on sales volume, will have no exposure to commodity risk. In practice, factors like competition and the availability of substitute products means that this policy does not cover all commodity price risks and a company may risk losing market share to other companies. For many businesses, commodity price risk can best be managed by entering into fixed price contracts with suppliers. Although this is relatively simple to arrange, the disadvantage might be higher costs and reduced flexibility.

One of the most obvious ways to reduce the exposure of a manufacturing company to commodity price risk is to use less of the commodity. This could be achieved through reformulating the product to use less of the material, introducing other materials in its place or designing a product so that the commodities embedded in it can easily be recycled or reused. You may have noticed that your favourite chocolate bar seems a lot smaller than you remember, or it doesn't taste quite the same. This is an example of "shrinkflation" as companies, in the face of rising commodity costs, look to improve their margins by offering a smaller or reformulated product at a similar price, not thinking that the customer will notice.

By its nature though, this reformulation of the product takes significant investment and by the time the new product is ready to be introduced the relative commodity prices may have changed, altering the commercial imperative. However, over the long term this could be a feasible strategy. Furthermore, optimising the process and distribution networks may allow commodity inventories to be reduced, lessening the commodity price risk exposure of the manufacturing company.

Ensuring access to resources higher up the supply chain helps to ensure physical supplies while also providing some control over the cost of a firms inputs. The advantage of such vertical integration is that it may reduce commodity price risk over the long term. The disadvantage is that a manufacturer may not be as efficient in running a business further up the supply chain, introducing higher costs.

A recent example of vertical integration is Delta Airlines, which in 2013 bought a refinery with the aim of reducing the airlines exposure to fuel price volatility and the cost of hedging that risk. By operating a refinery, Delta thought it would have an edge over the other airlines in hedging fuel costs. However, the biggest problem is that buying a refinery just isn't a great hedge against fuel prices because the real cost of jet fuel is the oil, not the refining. "It's as wrongheaded as buying a bakery to hedge against rising bread prices," according to Ed Hirs, an energy economist and lecturer at the University of Houston. "If you really want to hedge your bread price, then buy a wheat field."[107,108]

So what mistakes should you try and avoid when hedging your company's commodity exposure? Well, many companies fail to quantify their risk exposure to commodity prices. They often rely on ambiguous assumptions about price volatility and how and when movements in commodity prices impact on their bottom line. Often the first time it gains a company's attention is after a commodity "shock". A company should monitor and prepare for these "black swan" events by actively monitoring emerging commodity price pressures and by putting in place plans to address these high impact, low probability risks.

Many buyers don't take account of their full material cost breakdown. There can be considerable information asymmetry between buyers and sellers. Suppliers will have a full cost breakdown of the raw materials they supply, information that can be difficult for the buyer to obtain, especially when there is a degree of value added to the underlying commodity being supplied. Also, many firms do not try to get an overview of what is happening to the commodity prices that are essential to their business, with many companies relying on their raw material supplier as their main source of opinion on how commodity prices may develop.

A company should also consider Value at Risk (VaR) and Cash at Risk (CaR). The VaR is associated with the underlying value of the commodity that the buyer is seeking to manage in some way and is therefore a very short-term indicator. By its very nature, the VaR is very difficult to monitor and predict. However, since a commodity buyer will generally want to take delivery of the commodity at some point, a business also needs to consider the impact that its risk management strategy will have on cash flow. By considering CaR, businesses should bear in mind both the value of the commodity that they are purchasing and the sales price of the product that the commodity will be manufactured into over the lifetime of the hedging period.

Commodity price volatility may present an opportunity, as well as a threat. There is an argument for manufacturing companies to be more flexible in the way they purchase the commodities they need; for example, by being in a position to take advantage of a drop in prices. Set against this though, there is also a danger that companies might move too far away from being hedgers (managing their procurement risk) to being speculators; not to mention the time and resources that might be diverted away from their day to day job of actually making stuff.

The essential thing:

There are many ways in which companies can manage the supply chain and the financial risk of their exposure to commodities.

32) Commodity transportation

"If we see that our Ukrainian partners start illegally taking our gas from the export pipeline as it was in 2008, we will equally reduce the amount of supply as happened in 2008."

Vladimir Putin, President of Russia

Commodities can be heavy, fragile, dangerous and prone to high price volatility. Compared with other financial assets, such as shares and bonds, commodities are pretty difficult to move around. Some of them are dangerous (oil and gas, for example), while others degrade if not handled correctly (wheat and corn). The same concerns are relevant when storing commodities waiting to be used.

The primary means by which commodities are transported are pipeline, ship and rail. A few resources, including high-value agricultural and horticultural products and fine chemicals, tend to be air-freighted. Meanwhile, road transport plays a crucial end-point distribution role for petroleum and food.

Improving transport infrastructure, combined with lower costs, can be a major benefit to the consumers of commodities. Take the energy market, for instance. Before the introduction of super tankers, the oil market was made up of small regional markets, similar to today's gas markets. As costs fell and transport was made quicker and easier, pricing evolved towards a global benchmark, reducing price differences between regions.

The gas market could take a similar course to oil with the expansion of liquefied natural gas (LNG) supply. LNG involves cooling the gas to -260° Fahrenheit, which shrinks its volume by 600 times, thereby allowing for economical transportation in a specially designed tanker. However, by its very nature, this process is much more expensive than just sending the gas down a pipeline.

The Baltic Dry Index

The Baltic Dry Index (BDI) is a measure of the cost of shipping coal, iron ore and other dry cargoes, and it is often seen as a leading indicator of economic growth and commodity demand (some caution is advised here though). However, using the BDI to predict changes in commodity markets is a fool's game. The BDI is an indicator of short-term demand and supply for ships, and as so if rates rise it is because there are not enough ships available and there is too much demand for commodities at a particular moment in time. With the supply of ships being inelastic in the short term (ships can take many weeks to travel to the port where they are needed) and demand for commodities being volatile, any mismatch can easily be reflected in a sharp movement in the BDI.

As an example, imagine you have ten loads of iron ore and nine ships, and that every load of iron ore must be sent, no matter what, and every ship must be filled, no matter what.

> Imagine the bidding war between those ten iron ore consumers fighting over just nine ships. Shipping costs would rocket, since they all need to ship regardless of the cost.[109]

Whether by road, rail or by ship, the cost of fuel can have an impact on the cost of transporting commodities. For marine transport, the cost of fuel can account for more than 60% of the total operating cost. Bunker fuel, as it is known, is the residue left over from refining crude oil after the more valuable fuels have been extracted.[110]

Transport is also a risk, for both consumers and producers of commodities. Nowadays companies often hold limited stocks of commodities, instead relying on their delivery as and when needed. Although this has increased the economic efficiency of the global economy, it has also increased vulnerability to a transport related disruption. Poor investment in transport infrastructure can result in bottlenecks, potentially restricting supplies and/or resulting in higher commodity prices (see Chapter 38 for why climate change may lead to even more problems).

For a country so dependent on commodities, Brazil has woefully underinvested in the facilities to store them and transport them out of the country. Approximately 60% of its agricultural crops are sent by road, far across the country, from farms in the north to the country's biggest export terminal on the south coast, where there is a lack of grain silos for storage. In 2013, the country experienced a record harvest of soybeans.

However, the poor transport infrastructure led to queues of lorries stretching for more than 20 miles and ships waiting for approximately 40 days to dock. The result – crop wastage, higher costs for consumers and the cancellation of orders.[111]

Transporting certain commodities can also be very dangerous and lots of precautions need to be put in place to ensure there is no damage to the environment or danger to people. One of the most infamous disasters to hit the transport of commodities involved the Exxon Valdez, an oil tanker that spilled hundreds of thousands of barrels of crude oil off the coast of Alaska in 1989. In the immediate aftermath, as many as 250,000 seabirds, at least 2,800 sea otters, 300 harbour seals and an unknown number of salmon and herring died. The effects of the spill continued to be felt for many years afterwards. Since 2010, there were an estimated 23,000 US gallons of Valdez crude oil still in Alaska's sand and soil, breaking down at a rate estimated at less than 4% per year.[112]

Commodity transport routes also represent a geopolitical vulnerability. The Ukraine/Russia gas crisis, which came to a head in January 2009, resulted in 18 European countries reporting major falls or cut-offs in their gas supply. Even further back, the Suez crisis of 1956 was fought as trade routes, including the supply of energy and other commodities from the Middle East, through the Suez Canal were at risk (see Chapter 28 on geopolitics).

The essential thing:

Transporting commodities is fraught with difficulties, dangers and the risk that the commodity will be damaged.

33) Commodity trading firms

"As a trader you often walk on the blade. Be careful and don't step off."

Marc Rich

A small number of huge commodity trading firms dominate the production, transportation and trading of commodities. Virtually all commodities must undergo a variety of processes to transform them into things that we can actually consume. These transformations can be grouped into the following categories: space, time and form. Firms that are involved in commodity trading attempt to identify the most valuable of these transformations, undertake the transactions necessary to make these transformations and engage in the physical and operational actions necessary to carry them out.

The areas where commodities can be efficiently produced, such as fertile land or mineral deposits, are usually away from, and often far away from, where those who desire to consume them reside (see Chapter 32). This first transformation requires the transportation of commodities from where they are produced to the places they are consumed.

The timing of commodity production and consumption is often disjointed as well. This is most readily seen for agricultural commodities, which are often produced periodically (with a crop typically being harvested once a year) but consumed continuously throughout the year. These mismatches in the timing of production and consumption create a need to engage in temporal transformations, namely the storage of commodities. Stocks can be accumulated when supply is unusually high or demand is unusually low, and can then be drawn down upon when demand exceeds supply. Storage is a way of smoothing out the effects of these shocks on prices, consumption and production (see Chapter 3).

Finally, commodities must often undergo transformations in form in order to be suitable for final consumption or for use as an input in a process further down the value chain. For example, soybeans must be crushed to produce oil and meal that can be consumed, and crude oil must be refined into gasoline, diesel and other products.[113]

The leading independent energy trading houses – Vitol, Glencore, Trafigura, Mercuria and Gunvor – together handle more than enough oil to meet the import needs of the US, China and Japan. Agriculture is similar with Archer Daniels Midland (ADM), Bunge, Cargill and Dreyfus handling approximately half of the world's grain and soybean trade flows. Since the trade of diverse physical commodities requires matching numerous producers and consumers with diverse preferences, these commodity trading firms search to identify potential sellers and potential buyers and engage in bilateral transactions with them, adding value as they go.

Commodity trading firms do not tend to speculate on the outright direction of commodity prices, but instead aim to profit on the differential between the untransformed and transformed commodity. Commodity trading firms' core activities of buying, selling and transforming physical commodities takes place in what economists call bilateral "search" markets. The traders monitor supply and demand worldwide – data that they then use for arbitrage trading. At its most basic level, they may deploy people to count cocoa stocks in Ivory Coast, use infrared cameras to monitor oil levels in storage tanks or set up cameras to film coal stocks at Japanese power stations – all to determine the inventory fluctuations and price discrepancies through which they can profit.

According to a review by the Financial Times, the world's top 20 independent commodity traders posted a record net profit of $36.5bn in 2008, up approximately 1,600% from $2.1bn in 2000. Over the past decade, those 20 trading houses posted profits of $250bn – more than the world's top five carmakers combined.[114] What has caused their rapid growth? First, the economic boom in emerging countries after 2000 triggered a huge expansion in commodities trade. According to the US Department of Agriculture (USDA), trade in grain increased by 20.9% between 2001 and 2010, compared with an increase of just 1.9% between 1991 and 2000.

A second factor in the growth of the commodity trading firms involved a push into investing in commodity production, allowing them to profit from the super-cycle. Starting in the late 1980s, some trading firms began to invest in assets – oilfields, mines, farmland, refineries and smelters. When the price of commodities surged, so did the value of their assets.

Finally, tight markets are the third factor that greatly helped the rapid growth of the traders. When demand increased faster than supply, trading firms profited from the arbitrage opportunities offered by an abundance of price discrepancies between regions.

Given their size and importance to the global economy, are commodity trading firms now too big to fail? A report commissioned by the Global Financial Markets Association found that "it is unlikely that a large loss suffered by a single global commodity trading firm... poses a systemic threat to the broader financial system", adding that "the nature of commodity trading, and the structure and capital structures of commodity trading firms makes them substantially more robust to [a financial crisis] than systemically important financial institutions", like investment banks or big insurance companies. Indeed, two major trading houses have failed since 2000, without sparking disaster. Enron, which collapsed in 2001 after widespread accounting fraud, is the prime example. The entire merchant energy sector in the US imploded without disrupting the financial system or the trade in physical power and gas (see more on Enron in Chapter 45 about commodity market manipulation).

In recent years, competition has increased as traditional investment banks ventured into physical commodities trading, with major banks – including Morgan Stanley and J.P. Morgan – moving huge volumes of raw materials, on top of their traditional banking business of providing financial derivatives in commodities.

Banks getting involved in commodity trading, however, is nothing new. The Medici banking family was the most powerful financial institution in all of 15th century Europe. Soon after it was set up, it got into the textile industry, lending to English sheep farmers or wool merchants in return for lower prices, while also securing a near monopoly in the trade of alum.[115,116] However, following the financial crisis, regulators became increasingly worried about banks being involved with natural resources – if highly indebted financial institutions own big industrial assets, an accident may be a financial catastrophe, as well as an environmental one. Concern about reputation, the watchful eye of regulators, as well as a decline in revenue, prompted many investment banks to offload their physical commodity assets, and some even retreated from commodity trading altogether.

State owned commodity traders are starting to move into procuring and marketing commodities directly, bypassing the likes of Glencore and Cargill. These relatively new competitors are a threat to existing firms, in that many enjoy privileged access to the natural resources of the countries that own them. However, in contrast to private commodity trading firms that tend to be motivated by profit maximisation, state owned traders favour national interest and so may not be as equipped to spot and take advantage of commodity market imbalances.[117]

The essential thing:

A small number of very large commodity trading firms dominate the production, transportation and trading of commodities.

Want to know more? Visit my blog **Materials Risk** *and get email updates and analysis on what's really happening in commodities and commodity markets.*

34) Cartels and commodities

"Certain people enter cartels because of greed; then, because of greed, they try to get out of the cartels."

P. J. O'Rourke

Cartels and commodities are very close friends. A cartel is an explicit agreement among competing firms (or producers) to fix prices, marketing and production. They are much more common in oligopolistic industries, where the number of sellers is small and the product is relatively homogeneous.

Many commodities are geographically concentrated, resulting in the need for only a few players to restrict output to have an impact on the price. In the same way, geographical concentration means many of these countries are significantly dependent on revenues from commodities, increasing the incentive to act together and raise prices. For the cartel to work, the producers must control the supply in order to maintain an artificially high price. Collusion is easier to achieve when there is a relatively small number of producers in the market and a large number of customers, market demand is not too variable and the individual producers output is relatively easily monitored by the cartel organisation.

Cartels and oligopolistic industries in general have a delicate balancing act though. Get too tough with consumers by raising prices and you might see them looking for alternative sources of the commodity or substituting to a different commodity altogether. The entry of non-cartel producers into the market increases supply and puts downward pressure on the cartel's agreed on price.

Cartels also have a delicate internal balancing act. The higher the price, the greater the incentive for an individual member to break the agreement, resulting in higher supply and lower prices. This is most commonly described via the Prisoner's Dilemma game. Although price fixing is in the joint interests of all members of a cartel, it is not a profit maximising equilibrium for each individual producer in the cartel.

Shocks to either demand or supply tend to test the resolve of cartel agreements involving commodity producers. Shocks that require a price reduction tend to be accommodated relatively quickly by cartel members, since the downward adjustment is less costly in terms of market share. In contrast, raising prices is likely to involve a short run loss of market share for those cartel members that act first, resulting in a delay.

Cartels can only influence the spot price and the shape of the forward curve however (see Chapter 42). Long dated prices (beyond two years to an extent, but certainly beyond five years) are generally out of the cartel's control, as long as the cartel is not the marginal producer. In a market where the marginal producer is outside of the cartel, then the cartel would need to displace that producer by increasing production, requiring significant spare capacity (see Chapter 4 on commodity cost curves).

The most well known example of a commodity market in which cartel-like behaviour has a significant impact is the oil market. The Organisation of Petroleum Exporting Countries (OPEC) was set up in Baghdad, Iraq, in September 1960, to co-ordinate opposition to cuts in posted prices by the multinational oil companies. OPEC is a group of countries including some of the largest oil producers in the world. As of early 2015, OPEC included Algeria, Angola, Ecuador, Iran, Iraq, Kuwait, Libya, Nigeria, Qatar, the United Arab Emirates, Saudi Arabia and Venezuela, and together accounts for approximately 80% of global oil reserves and 45% of global oil production.

OPEC's overall objective is to achieve as high an oil price as possible, satisfying the interests of its members, but without snuffing out global demand for oil. OPEC generally looks to manage the oil price through formal or informal production quotas for each individual OPEC member. These quotas are determined by an individual producer's stated oil reserves. Already, this requirement provides an incentive for a producer to exaggerate their reserves in order to get away with producing more oil.

Each OPEC member must be able to trust the other OPEC members in order to stick to the agreement. If not, and if one producer starts producing more than their allocation (perhaps to take advantage of high oil prices or to finance some pressing need at home), then OPEC as a whole will produce more oil than they agreed to, pushing down oil prices and making all other members worse off.

Saudi Arabia, being the largest producer, has traditionally held the role of "swing producer" within OPEC. A commodity supplier in this position tends to possess significant spare production capacity and is able to adjust commodity supply at minimal additional cost in order to help balance the market and adjust prices.

Cartel-like behaviour doesn't just happen in the oil market, however. De Beers is well known for its monopolist practices throughout the 20th century, whereby it used its dominant position to manipulate the international diamond market. It persuaded independent producers to join its single channel monopoly, flooding the market with diamonds similar to those of producers who refused to join the cartel. It then purchased and stockpiled the diamonds produced by other manufacturers in order to control prices through supply. In 2000, the cartel changed after diamond producers in Russia, Canada and Australia decided to distribute diamonds outside the De Beers distribution channel. In addition, rising awareness of blood diamonds (those produced in areas involved in civil war, such as Sierra Leone; see Chapter 41) forced De Beers to limit the sale of its own mined products. The end result was that De Beers market share fell from as high as 90% in the 1980s to less than 40% in 2012.

Not all commodities are likely to feature this kind of manipulative behaviour however. Commodity production needs to be concentrated in the hands of a very small number of significant producers in order to enable collective decisions on prices and output to take place. For many commodities, wide geographical dispersion and the resulting political and commercial differences mean that cartels are far less likely to form.

The essential thing:

Cartels can act to restrict output and raise commodity prices in the short-term, to the detriment of consumers... but they are inherently unstable.

35) Technology and innovation

"Where oil is first found, in the final analysis, is in the minds of men."

Wallace Pratt

High commodity prices provide the incentive for technical innovation. Innovations, once introduced, may lead to higher yields from agriculture, more oil being extracted from offshore wells and deeper and deeper mines to extract metals and minerals. All of which could eventually lead to rising commodity supplies. High commodity prices may also lead to innovation on the demand side too. High energy prices, for example, may discourage consumers from using a particular energy inefficient product. This acts an incentive for companies to redesign their products to become more energy efficient and less resource intensive.

One of the most widely known innovations in commodity production is a technique known as hydraulic fracturing, or fracking. Back in 2004, the book "High Noon for Natural Gas" lamented the lack of planning for the soon-to-bite shortage of domestically produced North American natural gas. Just a few years later, the author's prophecies appeared to be coming true with US natural gas prices rising to $14 per million British thermal units (mBtu).[118] Soon afterwards, natural gas prices collapsed. A glut of new "unconventionally" extracted supplies hit the market as hitherto unobtainable gas, thought forever locked into impermeable shale rock formations, became easily extractable using cutting-edge hydraulic fracturing and horizontal drilling techniques. These techniques were once expensive and highly experimental. Today, they are conventional and often cheaper than more established techniques (see Chapter 36 for more on the technological innovations behind the shale revolution).

Nickel (a crucial input in stainless steel production) is also a prime example of how innovation can respond to high prices. Prior to the mid-2000s, most of the world's nickel supply came from mines that were controlled by large global mining firms, such as Russia's Norilsk Nickel. With a dearth of investment in project expansions over the prior decade, nickel mines were becoming increasingly depleted. These supply concerns, coupled with China's accelerating pace of industrialisation, resulted in nickel prices soaring to a peak of $51,800 per tonne in 2007, marking a fourfold increase in less than three years. But the world did not run out of nickel and prices did not keep spiralling higher. Instead, record high prices incentivised Chinese stainless steel companies to investigate lower cost alternatives.

Technological improvements eventually enabled the widespread adoption of nickel pig iron (NPI), a substitute made out of laterite nickel ore, coking coal, sand and gravel. The global stainless steel industry had long known that laterite nickel deposits, found in Indonesia and the Philippines, could be refined into a substance which contained relatively low levels of nickel. The first forays into refining laterite ore into NPI were prohibitively expensive and created excess pollution from the inefficient blast furnaces. In 2006, the marginal costs of NPI production was approximately $20,000 per tonne, compared to nickel prices that had hovered around $10,000 per tonne for much of the previous ten years. It was just not economic to produce the lower-grade version of nickel and the big multinational mining companies essentially ignored the resource.

Yet as nickel prices rose steadily and major Chinese stainless steel producers were forced to think creatively and to explore alternative sources of supply. Suddenly, NPI began to look more economically attractive. Chinese companies began testing methods to make the process more efficient. As smelters along the eastern coast of China began swapping their production of other alloys to that of NPI, techniques improved. With the sudden influx of new supply, nickel prices plummeted.

The real catalyst for change however, came in late 2010 with the discovery of the rotary kiln electric furnace, which improved efficiency and halved production costs of NPI to approximately $12,000 per tonne. By replacing blast furnaces with this new invention, Chinese stainless steel companies found that they could use less energy and extract more nickel content.[119]

We've highlighted technological improvements in energy and metal supply but what about food? Norman Borlaug introduced several revolutionary innovations in the 1960s and became known as the Father of the Green Revolution. First, he and his colleagues crossbred thousands of wheat varieties from around the world to produce new ones that were resistant to rust, a destructive plant pest. This innovation alone raised wheat yields by 20-40%.[120] Second, he crafted so-called dwarf wheat varieties, which were smaller than the old shoulder-high varieties that bent in the wind and touched the ground (thereby becoming impossible to harvest with modern machinery). The new waist high dwarfs stayed upright and held up huge loads of grain. The yields were boosted even further. Third, he devised a technique known as "shuttle breeding". This involved growing two successive plantings each year instead of the usual one, testing it in different regions of Mexico. The availability of two test generations of wheat each year cut by half the number of years required for breeding new varieties. Moreover, because the two regions were characterised by distinctly different climatic conditions, the resulting new early-maturing, rust-resistant varieties were broadly adapted to many latitudes, altitudes and soil types. This wide adaptability proved invaluable and wheat yields rocketed further.

How successful were Borlaug's efforts? India is an excellent example. In pre-Borlaug 1963, wheat grew there in sparse, irregular strands. It was harvested by hand and was susceptible to rust disease. The maximum yield was 800 lb per acre. By 1968, thanks to Borlaug's varieties, the wheat grew densely packed, was resistant to rust and the maximum yield had risen almost eight-fold to 6000 lb of wheat per acre.

Even in agriculture the deployment of new technology is not uniform. For crops that have a natural annual cycle, like corn, new methods can be introduced and tested on a regular interval, but for others like cocoa (where trees take 3-4 years before germinating) the opportunity to introduce innovation, and so improve yields, is more limited.

The essential thing:

High commodity prices encourage investment in new production techniques (or the introduction of those techniques previously thought to be uneconomic) and for companies to redesign their products to become more energy efficient and less resource intensive.

36) The shale revolution

"There is only one rule of thumb in fracturing: that there are no rules of thumb in fracturing."

Reservoir Stimulation

One of the most widely known innovations in commodity production in recent years is a technique known as hydraulic fracturing, or fracking. At a basic level, this involves drilling down into the Earth and then injecting water and other materials into the rock at high pressure to unlock oil and natural gas.

One of the biggest myths surrounding fracking is that it is actually a new technology. It was in 1862, during the battle of Fredericksburg VA, where civil war veteran Col. Edward A. L. Roberts saw what could be accomplished when firing explosive artillery into a narrow canal that obstructed the battlefield. Modern day hydraulic fracturing began in the 1940s, when in 1947 Floyd Farris of Stanolind Oil and Gas began a study on the relationship between oil and gas production output and the amount of pressurised treatment being used on each well.[121] What is often forgotten, or at least misunderstood, is the impact that horizontal drilling has had on the success of the shale revolution. And even this isn't a new innovation. It wasn't until the 1990s that George P. Mitchell created a technique that took hydraulic fracturing and combined it with horizontal drilling.

When drilling into a hydrocarbon-bearing formation 100 feet thick, vertical drilling allows an operator to drill through that 100 feet of rock, limiting the potential recovery to whatever oil or gas would flow into that length of pipe. Horizontal drilling, on the other hand, allows these operators to drill for a mile or more, horizontally, through this rock formation, multiplying the expected well recovery rates many times over.

Advanced horizontal drilling technology also produces good results for the environment. A single horizontal well can replace the need to drill a dozen or more vertical wells to access a similar level of resource. For the environment, this means less air pollution, less water usage and disposal needs, and less land impacted to produce a comparable amount of oil and natural gas.[122]

A glut of new "unconventionally" extracted gas and oil supplies, previously thought forever locked into impermeable shale rock formations in the US, became easily extractable using cutting-edge hydraulic fracturing and horizontal drilling techniques. These techniques were once expensive and highly experimental. Today, they are conventional and often cheaper than more established techniques.

The amount of gas and oil produced from a new well has actually risen significantly as producers have improved their technology and methods. The increases in production with a fixed number of rigs and the rise in output from new wells imply two things. First, the marginal cost of new shale wells is most likely decreasing as firms become quicker and more efficient at drilling them. Second, that producers are in fact getting better at finding the most productive spots and at coaxing more oil out of them.

The extraction techniques used in shale extraction, hydraulic fracturing and horizontal drilling, have proved controversial. Vast amounts of water mixed with chemicals are used, which could, it is feared, contaminate underground aquifers and deplete water resources. Attention has also concentrated on the risk that fracking causes earthquakes. Although fracking has caused seismic activity, these events have been infrequent and of a lower magnitude compared with those caused by conventional oil production or mining. Meanwhile some contend that fracking will extend the world's reliance on fossil fuels.[123]

As with any source of commodities, whether it is solar power or deep sea oil, drilling to actually get to the stuff requires using lots of other commodities. The process involved in fracking is no different. Two of the commodities to benefit have been sand and guar. Demand for sand, or frac-sand (durable high-purity quartz sand used to help produce petroleum fluids and prop up man-made fractures in shale rock formations), surged as oil and gas flows have increased. The derivatives of guar gum are used in several industries, including textiles, pharmaceuticals, food processing and oil extraction. But it was its unique binding, thickening and emulsifying qualities that made it especially suitable for fracking. Demand from fracking has caused the price of guar to rise ten-fold in the five years to 2014.[124]

Is the US the next Middle East? It's not likely. Doubts have surfaced as to whether the US shale industry will hit the geological buffers sooner rather than later. A 2013 US Energy Department report estimated "proven reserves" of shale oil – those that can be recovered economically today – at only approximately ten billion barrels. In contrast, the proven reserves from just three Middle East nations – Saudi Arabia, Kuwait and the United Arab Emirates – amount to more than 460 billion barrels. Other countries, from the UK to Poland and China, keen to increase energy security, reduce energy costs and climate impacts have sought to utilise shale gas extraction techniques. However, environmental concerns, high costs, regulatory hurdles and more challenging geological formations compared to the US has slowed its development (see Chapter 40 for more on how water supply is critical to fracking).

Concerns over the long-term success of shale is, in part, driven by the sharp drop off in production rates observed at many existing oil and gas wells. Fracked wells are short-lived, with a well's output typically declining from more than 1,000 barrels a day to 100 barrels in just a few years. Therefore, new wells must be drilled frequently to maintain production. While wells currently pumping can survive low market prices because they have already incurred start-up and drilling costs, lower oil prices may diminish the incentive to invest in new wells.

In contrast to conventional oil production where the time lag between the decision to invest and oil being produced is measured in years, the lead time in shale production is just weeks. Short production lags and high decline rates means that there is a close relationship between investment and production. The consequence of these characteristics is that the short-run responsiveness of shale oil to changes in the price of oil will be far greater than that for conventional oil, potentially dampening oil price volatility (see Chapter 22). As prices fall, investment and drilling activity will decline and production will soon follow, and vice versa as prices recover.

The essential thing:

Hydraulic fracturing and horizontal drilling have revolutionised oil and gas production in the US.

*Want to know more? Visit my blog **Materials Risk** and get email updates and analysis on what's really happening in commodities and commodity markets.*

37) Subsidies and taxes

"The IMF provides five trillion reasons for acting on fossil fuel subsidies. Protecting the poor and the vulnerable is crucial to the phasing down of these subsidies, but the multiple economic, social and environmental benefits are long and legion."

Christiana Figueres, the UN's climate change chief

Commodities are politically sensitive, often with perverse and adverse consequences. Governments frequently subsidise commodity prices, particularly energy and agricultural ones, in the name of providing a benefit to their poorest citizens in the shape of cheaper fuel and food. More commonly though, especially for oil producing countries, it is also to provide a visible example of the benefit of their carbon wealth, while in autocratic regimes they have been used to quell unrest from the poor and to keep the elite on side. What is striking about food and fossil fuel subsidies is that they are often promoted in the name of the environment or equality. In reality, however, they do little to achieve these goals and often have the opposite effect.

According to the International Monetary Fund (IMF), approximately $550 billion a year is spent on energy subsidies. Half is spent by governments in the Middle East and North Africa, where on average it is worth approximately 20% of government revenues. Rather than benefiting the poor, the proceeds flow to the car-driving urban elite. In the typical emerging economy, the richest fifth of households swallow up 40% of the benefits of fuel subsidies; the poorest fifth get only 7%.

On a global basis, the effects of subsidies are also damaging – all this over consumption also results in increased carbon emissions. According to the International Energy Agency (IEA), eliminating fossil fuel subsidies alone would reduce global carbon emissions by 6% by 2020.

Energy and food subsidies also dampen the responsiveness of global demand to high fuel prices, resulting in commodity prices that are higher than they would otherwise be. With subsidies to fossil fuels more than four times higher than those paid to renewable energy, they also hold back investment in cleaner forms of energy production (see Chapter 10 on low carbon energy sources).[125]

Agricultural subsidies, meanwhile, sometimes seek to benefit consumers at the expense of producers, especially in poor countries, and sometimes seek to benefit producers at the expense of consumers, particularly in rich countries. India's policies currently try to do both, by rationing grain to consumers at artificially low prices, while simultaneously suffering excess supply because farmers are paid high prices. Farmers in India are also subsidised via the cost of agricultural inputs – electricity, water and fertiliser – to the detriment of the environment. The government has purchased huge stockpiles of rotting rice and wheat, while the limited amount available to consumers is distributed in ways that are corrupt and inconsistent with the stated goal of helping the poor.[126]

The reasons for government support vary from environmental to cultural. Food security and self-sufficiency has been a deep-rooted cause, and after the sharp rise in food prices in 2008-09, some countries increased their support for the agricultural sector to avoid running out of food. In emerging economies, subsidies have tended to rise as government income has increased and policy priorities have become increasingly concentrated on agricultural and rural development.

The poorest tend to suffer disproportionately from the distortions that such interventions create. Egypt, for example, used to spend seven times more on fuel subsidies than on health. Cheap fuel encourages the development of heavy industry, rather than the job-rich light manufacturing that offers far more people a route out of poverty.

Meanwhile cheap food and fuel have a number of side effects, including encouraging over consumption, discouraging investment in infrastructure, threatening resource security by increasing the reliance on imported food and fuel, disproportionate benefits to the middle class and rich and higher budget deficits as the cost to maintain subsidies balloons. However, once subsidies are in place, they are extraordinarily difficult to remove. When world commodity prices rise, citizens who are accustomed to the domestic price being set in the market are more likely to accept the reality that government officials cannot insulate them from the price shock. However, people who are accustomed to administratively established food and energy prices tend to hold their government responsible.

The sudden removal of subsidies frequently ends in disaster, often resulting in a violent backlash followed by a political climb down. Nigeria's announcement to end domestic fuel subsidies in 2012 led to an overnight doubling of prices and national strikes – which evolved into further protests against endemic corruption. In response, the government reduced rather than removed these subsidies. The sharp drop in the oil price in late 2014 has given many economies where domestic fuel subsidies are in use an excellent opportunity to begin scaling them back, without prompting a backlash.[127]

It isn't just less developed economies that use subsidies. Many less developed economies were squeezed out of the global food production system by low agriculture prices that were the result of excess capacity in the US and Europe. Big subsidies over the past several decades have helped create this excess capacity, which made a significant number of family and small farms in Africa and Latin America uneconomical. Land use could be more efficiently allocated by removing these trade barriers, resulting in lower agriculture prices, but high enough to allow these farmers to earn a profit.

On the other side of subsidies, taxes represent a gain to a government and a loss to the consumer or business. Taxes tend to be used by governments to tax consumption and here they are generally placed on the consumption of energy (particularly transport fuel, but also heating too). One reason governments use to justify taxes on fuel is to account for the associated environmental cost. These negative externalities, as they are known, include carbon dioxide (which contributes to global warming), the release of other toxins and harmful substances like carbon monoxide and fine particulates and the cost of road congestion (see Chapter 38 on commodities and climate change).

Taxes on fuel can vary significantly between countries. In many European countries, tax represents approximately 60% of the cost of filling up a car. While in many oil producing countries, almost no tax at all is levied. High fuel taxes impact the way consumers react to a change in the price of oil. In contrast to high fuel tax countries, lower oil prices are felt more visibly at the pump in low tax countries, encouraging consumers to drive more or to upgrade their vehicle – perhaps to a less fuel efficient Sports Utility Vehicle (SUV).

The main reason for the difference in taxation is population density. Countries in Western Europe have very high population densities and this allows the use of mass transportation and higher taxes on transport fuel; compare this with the US or Canada with low population densities. Finally, smaller nations tend to have less efficient distribution systems and so suffer from poor economies of scale.[128]

The essential thing:

Governments can use fiscal policy (subsidies and taxes) to influence both commodity production and consumption... but each tends to have perverse and sometimes unintended consequences.

38) Climate change

"Houses were shut tight, and cloth wedged around doors and windows, but the dust came in so thinly that it could not be seen in the air, and it settled like pollen on the chairs and tables, on the dishes."

John Steinbeck

"EACH DAY HUMBLE SUPPLIES ENOUGH ENERGY TO MELT 7 MILLION TONS OF GLACIER!"

Gasoline advertisement in LIFE magazine, 1962

The weather can have a significant impact on both the supply and demand for commodities. But what if the current variability and extremes in the weather are nothing in comparison to what the future could hold?

Rising global temperatures are often assumed to be unambiguously negative for the output of agricultural commodities. However, although there is plenty of debate about the causes and impacts of climate change, even among those who agree it is happening, there are also good reasons to believe that some crops could actually benefit.

First, an increase in the amount of carbon dioxide (CO_2) in the atmosphere can actually help some crops to flourish. For example, some studies suggest that a doubling of CO_2 could increase the yields of wheat and soybeans by approximately 30% and of corn by approximately 10%. In fact, the 50% increase in CO_2 concentrations over the last hundred years or so may have already contributed to the growth in crop yields over that time.[129]

Second, an increase in temperatures could allow crops to grow more quickly than at present. Milder and shorter winters in northern countries, such as Canada and Russia, could allow substantially increased grain production because more of these countries' vast territories would be suitable for planting. The crops would therefore be subject to a lower risk of frost damage during the winter.

Although higher temperatures mean that overall rainfall may increase, some countries may become too hot and arid for cultivation, reducing the available planting area and damaging yields. This is a particular concern in regions that are already prone to droughts. One implication is that the impacts on crops such as cocoa, which are mainly grown in Africa, are more likely to be negative than the impacts on cereals. In addition, climate change is likely to increase the frequency of extreme events such as floods, hurricanes, droughts and diseases. These types of events tend to lead to a dramatic increase in the volatility of agricultural commodity markets. This increased volatility in turn could lead to a permanent increase in the risk premium in prices, reflecting the greater supply uncertainty.

Overall, the impact of climate change on agricultural commodities could go either way. Volatility in prices is likely to be higher, but, often, increases in temperature and in CO_2 concentration may actually boost supply and result in lower prices over the longer term.

Climate change may also affect the transportation and logistics involved in supplying commodities. Future growth in trade with emerging economies may expose more developed economies to regions more vulnerable to climate impacts. With a significant proportion of commodities and resources transported by sea freight, coastal infrastructure, such as ports, are likely to be impacted by sea level rises and an increasing intensity and frequency of extreme weather events, which could cause temporary or permanent closures or damage. Shortages and uncertainty over the supplies of raw materials could lead to higher and more volatile prices. You only need to look back to the Thai floods of 2011 to see the scale of the potential impact. Back then, flooding resulted in the shutdown of at least half of the country's hard disk drive (HDD) production capacity, one quarter of global capacity, resulting in a tripling in HDD prices.

Apparel/clothing is an essential product at risk from climate change. Their imports are threatened because suppliers are particularly vulnerable to climate change; cotton, for instance, uses large volumes of water to be produced.

As climate change intensifies, a wider range of commodities are likely to be affected, resulting in increased volatility. With supply chains increasingly integrated, the impact of commodity price volatility will be transmitted more rapidly. Volatile and rising prices will increasingly affect profitability for those companies with resource intensive and climate change exposed supply chains, and those less able to manage and control their input costs.

The essential thing:

Climate change could lead to more volatile commodity prices.

39) Will fixing the climate leave fossil fuels stranded?

"We're not going to be able to burn it all."

President Obama

How much of the Earth's fossil fuel reserves (oil, coal and gas etc.) will eventually be burnt? It is an essential question that energy producers and explorers need to consider when deciding to invest in exploration and additional production for tomorrow. For if policy makers acted on their expressed belief in the science of climate change, this investment could prove to be a disastrous waste of resources with the amount of oil, gas and coal that can be safely used already discovered.

Energy plays a central role in the global economy, in particular fossil fuels – coal, oil and natural gas – and the power that has been generated from them. Unfortunately, fossil fuel use has also been a major source of carbon emissions. Therefore, addressing climate change will invariably require a reduction or change in fossil fuel use, potentially reducing the value of those fossil fuel resources.

In 2010, governments around the world agreed that emissions should be kept at a level intended to prevent an increase in global average temperatures of more than 2°C above pre-industrial levels, equating to a CO_2 level of 450 particles per million (ppm). By some estimates, the total emissions of carbon dioxide between 2013 and 2050 needed to deliver that outcome, at 80% probability, would be 900 billion tonnes. However, according to the International Energy Agency (IEA), existing reserves of fossil fuels would, if burnt without capture of the carbon dioxide emissions, release 2,860 billion tonnes – approximately three times the global carbon budget. Burning this stock of fossil reserves, without any further additions to it, would push the global average temperature up by well over 3°C.[130]

With approximately two-thirds of their reserves set to become fictional, the fossil fuel industry could stand to lose $28 trillion of gross revenues over the next two decades, compared with business as usual. If their assets are left unexploited or decline in value because of actions to reduce the threat of climate change, these unexploited assets are then deemed "stranded". The energy business is entirely familiar with the concept of stranded assets, where all sorts of reserves are identified, but cannot be developed due to regulatory, technical and/or economic reasons. Stranded assets can include physical assets (such as power plants) or resources (such as oil).[131]

The impact of efforts by governments to achieve a temperature increase of no more than 2°C will depend upon the type of policies introduced. Stranding is a function of changed consumption and expectations, which are in turn affected by changes in policy, pricing, technology and behaviour. A climate related policy change that causes this could include: consumption taxes that suppress demand and thus reduce wholesale prices, production taxes which could raise costs, regulation that restricts development and innovation or efficiency policy which suppresses demand. The range of policy options can lead to different responses from producers, consumers and investors, which could affect the total net stranding cost and how that cost is spread.

Although many institutional investors are persuaded by this argument, there are significant barriers to overcome if the trend is to be widely embraced. Fossil fuel investment meets numerous institutional investor imperatives that are not currently found in other sectors of the economy, specifically overall scale, liquidity, value growth and dividend yield. Other alternative investments, with similar characteristics, must be found to encourage this transition to take place.[132]

Action by investors to divert funds away from climate causing companies won't necessarily have any material impact on climate change, however, because the really big oil reserves don't belong to companies, but governments instead. Given their significant strategic value, many countries have sought to control the production, price and value of their energy producing assets (see Chapter 28 for more on geopolitics and commodity markets). Globally, governments own 50-70% of global oil, gas and coal resources, as well as collect taxes and royalties on the portion they do not own. According to HSBC, only four of the top 20 owners of oil reserves are private companies which might be hurt by divestment (BP, Shell, Exxon and Lukoil), and none are in the top ten.[133] [134]

Remember, fossil fuel production will continue as long as there is demand. If the world used less oil, coal and other fossil fuels, less would be extracted. Just like the limits to growth in agricultural and energy production advanced by Malthus and Hubbert et al (see Chapter 25 and Chapter 26), the need to constrain greenhouse gas emissions in order to tackle global warming could be characterised as a new form of Malthusian limit. But this too could be overcome by shifting to a low carbon economy (see Chapter 10 on renewable energy).

The essential thing:

Burning all of the world's fossil reserves is incompatible with efforts to slow down climate change.

*Want to know more? Visit my blog **Materials Risk** and get email updates and analysis on what's really happening in commodities and commodity markets.*

40) Water

"The marginal cost of water is rising around the world. Previously, water was treated as a free raw material. Now, companies are realising it can damage their brand, their credibility, their credit rating and their insurance costs. That applies to a computer chipmaker and a food company as much as a power generator or a petrochemicals company."

Christopher Gasson, Global Water Intelligence

"We never know the worth of water 'til the well is dry."

English proverb

In theory, water should never be in short supply. Water covers approximately 71% of the earth's surface, however, 97% of it is too salty for productive use. Of the 2.5% that is usable freshwater, 70% is in icecaps, and much of the rest is in the ground. This leaves just 0.007% of the earth's water supply in the form of readily accessible freshwater, and like arable land, that freshwater is not evenly distributed.

According to the UN, agriculture accounts for 70% of global water use, compared with 22% for industry and just 8% for domestic users. These proportions vary by country, but the problem water scarcity poses for businesses in many parts of the world is that it pits the two biggest users, farmers and factories, against each other.

Everything we eat, whether it is the eggs and toast you had for breakfast, the salad you had for lunch or the steak you had for dinner, indirectly consumes massive quantities of water in its production. For example, it takes 547 litres of water to produce 1 kg of potatoes, 1,534 litres per kg of corn and 2,191 litres to produce 1 kg of soybeans. But these numbers pale into insignificance once you consider the amount of water needed to produce meat. To produce just 1 kg of beef requires 109,671 litres of water.[135]

Water is essential in the production of a range of different commodities and not just agricultural commodities. Energy runs on water. In fact, among industries, the global energy sector is the world's largest water user. Almost all forms of energy production and power generation (whether it be nuclear, oil, coal or gas) depend upon water for their operations. It takes 38 litres of water to power one house for one month from gas (~1,000 kWh), up to 2,100 litres of water from coal and up to 31,000 litres of water from oil.[136]

Nearly 93% of the Middle East's onshore oil reserves are exposed to medium to extremely high overall water quantity risk, according to the World Resources Institute (WRI). In addition to these supply concerns, energy companies in the Middle East face two primary water risks. First, inadequate desalination or other water infrastructure can disrupt ongoing projects. Second, domestic desalination consumes oil resources that could have been exported to customers around the world. In Saudi Arabia, for example, oil is sold to power and desalination plants at approximately $4 a barrel, but can be exported for significantly more.[137]

The burgeoning shale extraction industry is also at risk from water scarcity. Shale and tight gas drillers use a small percentage of water compared to other industrial users in the US, but individual wells need large volumes of water during short periods of time for hydraulic fracturing. These short but intense demands add up and can threaten to displace other water users. Over time, freshwater availability in shale development areas could decline as demand from homes and farms start competing with hydraulic fracturing operations. According to the WRI in the US, more than 50% of reserves of shale and tight gas - gas trapped in especially hard, non-permeable rock - are in areas of medium to extremely high baseline water stress. These concerns extend beyond the US, too. In the ten countries with the largest shale and tight gas reserves, 60% of the reserves are in areas facing medium to extremely high baseline water stress.

Why is water essential to the mining industry? Well, at a basic level drinking quality water is required to support towns that have developed in remote areas, often home to mining staff. Water is also favoured in mineral processing because it is a low cost and energy efficient way of transporting materials between processes - including disposing of, or storing, waste materials. Water is also a very efficient medium for supplying chemicals and mixing materials, and it is an essential ingredient for some chemical processes. The global mining industry's spending on water increased from $3.4bn in 2009 to nearly $10bn in 2013.[138] Costs are likely to keep rising. According to Moody, 70% of the six biggest global miners' existing mines are in countries where water stress is rated as a high or moderate risk, along with two-thirds of projects being developed.

Although it may seem anathema to put a price on something as essential to human life as water, the arguments for doing so could be compelling, especially in areas of water stress. Looking ahead into the next quarter century, clean drinkable water is expected to become scarcer as the human population grows and climate change shifts the shorelines and weather patterns. As with other commodities, price can theoretically help manage demand while providing an incentive to increase supply. As weather patterns shift, water could be transported to areas of high demand from areas where there is excess supply. At present, water use tends to be tightly regulated at a local level, while the cost of transporting water over long distance is prohibitively high.

As water stress becomes increasingly common and its value for agriculture and industry, in particular, rises, then business and governments across the world may adapt. In the not too distant future there could well be a globally integrated market for freshwater, including futures and spot pricing, and perhaps with fleets of water tankers and storage facilities. In fact, the trading of water rights already exists in Australia, an area of acute water stress but also high demand from agriculture. During the 2007/08 drought, water prices reached a peak of $1,200 per million litres (ML). As rain returned and supplies were replenished, prices subsequently fell to $4 per ML in 2010/11.[139]

A number of factors complicate ascribing value to water as a commodity, however. For instance, although bottled water is traded across international borders and offers a transparent and (theoretically) easily observable price for a unit of water, the implicit value of water itself is delinked from its price in that the value of water in sustaining life may be so much greater than a market price can truly capture. In addition, water assets generally do not have clear and transferable ownership title – rarely can one individual claim rights to a specific reservoir or lake – thus making it difficult to trade water assets, as opposed to more conventional commodities. To be traded on the global commodities exchanges, a resource has to be transferable (even if you are selling future rights to it) and transparently priced.[140]

The essential thing:

Water is an essential natural resource used in the production of commodities. Although "free" at the point of consumption, it is increasingly scarce, threatening the supply of a range of commodities.

41) Sustainability

"That diamond upon your finger, say how came it yours?"

"Thou'lt torture me, to leave unspoken that which, to be spoke, would torture thee."

Shakespeare's Cymbeline

How do you know if the metals in your mobile phone are not perpetuating conflict in the Democratic Republic of Congo, or that your coffee is not destroying the ecosystem in Colombia? The "sustainability" movement in commodities has grown over the past few years as companies and industries have shifted from the initial denial that any problems had anything to do with themselves.

Today, environmental change and degradation are presenting new challenges to business-as-usual assumptions about future resource extraction, production, processing and consumption – whether directly, through scarcities of specific inputs such as water, or indirectly, through social and political opposition. Environmental impacts include biodiversity loss, deforestation, soil erosion and land degradation to air and water pollution and global climate change.

One of the commodities most often associated with environmental damage is palm oil. Palm oil is the most widely used vegetable oil in the world and is found in half of all packaged products on the supermarket shelves, from shampoo to detergents. Yet the far-reaching impacts of its production are not widely known. Much of Indonesia's forests have been cleared to make way for palm oil output. Between 1967 and 2000, land designated for palm oil plantations in Indonesia rocketed from less than 2000 sq. km to more than 30,000 sq. km. Space for the expanding plantations is often created by draining and burning peat land, which in turn sends plumes of carbon emissions in to the atmosphere. Although, not just attributed to palm oil, today, Indonesia ranks behind the US and China in terms of total man-made greenhouse gas emissions.

Conflict minerals are minerals mined in conditions where armed conflict and human rights abuses occur. The term commonly applies to the extraction of four important minerals: Tungsten, Tantalum, Tin and Gold – 3TG for short. The minerals are used in a variety of applications that we use every day. Among an array of other applications, tungsten is used in the vibration of mobile phones, tantalum in vacuum tube filaments, tin is used in glass making and gold in electronic components.

The Democratic Republic of Congo has been at the centre of the trade in conflict minerals, with approximately $1.2 billion in minerals estimated to have been smuggled out of the country by armed groups on an annual basis. In response, the Dodd-Frank securities law created reporting obligations for companies publicly listed in the US. The Dodd-Frank law and electronics industry audits helped create a two-tier market for the 3Ts from Congo and the region. Minerals that do not go through conflict-free programs now sell for 30-60% less, reducing profits for armed groups trying to sell them. As businesses begin to comply with Dodd-Frank, they are requiring suppliers to conduct conflict-free audits and trace the sources of their minerals much more carefully. This has shrunk markets for untraceable conflict minerals.[141]

Sustainability doesn't just mean avoiding environmental damage or conflict, it can relate to improving society too. Take the example of cocoa, the essential ingredient for chocolate. Cocoa is mainly grown by smallholder farmers in the tropical areas of Africa, Latin America and Asia. As demand for chocolate increases, the growers need to be paid more if they are to be encouraged to remain a supplier to the chocolate industry. However, the sheer poverty of many farmers in West Africa, which produces the bulk of the world's cocoa, threatens to drive them away. The levels of growers' incomes provides little incentive for the younger generation to farm cocoa. Farmers in the Ivory Coast, the largest producer of cocoa, reportedly made 50 cents a day in 2014, far below the international poverty line of $2. Farmers only get a small fraction – 6.6% – of the chocolate bar's value, a result of a supply chain dominated by a few big players. This concentration further weakens the position of farmers.[142]

The low income afforded to cocoa growers stores up problems for the future. First, cocoa is a particularly volatile commodity with concentrated production and demand closely attuned to economic growth. This volatility creates uncertainty, which combined with low incomes, long production lead times and the impact of climate change means there is little incentive to invest in raising yields (see Chapter 22 on volatility, Chapter 35 on technology and Chapter 23 on adding value).

One way in which poverty in cocoa and other commodity supply chains is being tackled is through Fairtrade. The rationale behind Fairtrade is that producers of commodities subject to price volatility should be protected through the payment of a minimum price to cover living and production costs, a price which adjusts whenever the market shifts above a minimum threshold. In addition to this, traders should pay workers a "social premium" of approximately 5-10% to pay for development and technical assistance. Chocolate companies and others are also working with farmers directly to encourage sustainable sources, such as planting disease resistant varieties.[143]

Sustainability isn't just about Corporate Social Responsibility (CSR), it can bring real benefits to a company and its reputation if the right steps are taken. What happens if a civil war breaks out in the region in which you source commodities essential to your business? What if poor infrastructure means that when crops eventually get to the port their quality has deteriorated? What will be the impact on prices and the margin you can make if farmers feel that there is no incentive to invest in the future production of a commodity that is essential to your business?

The rising demand for sustainable raw materials has increased the call for retailers, manufacturers, commodities traders and producers to certify that commodities are extracted or grown according to certain standards. Some commodities are doing better than others. According to the International Institute for Sustainable Development, 40% of coffee production is now certified as sustainable, while 3% or less of cotton, bananas, sugar and soybean production is certified.[144] But certification has had its downsides too. The myriad of standards has confused consumers and farmers, and has often led to fraud and false auditing. There is also criticism among some social activists and farmers that standards and certification programmes are expensive tools that fail to reduce poverty. Meanwhile, certification may require farmers to make investments and changes that do not necessarily lead to high enough prices of the commodity to cover the costs. They may help farmers to be slightly more socially and environmentally sustainable, but nevertheless they remain mired in poverty.

The essential thing:

Environmental damage, civil unrest and poverty are all risks to future commodity supplies, company profits and reputation.

42) Commodity futures markets

"The brilliance of commodities futures is that they turn all of those physical goods, those valuable assets that you can touch and even smell, into paper that can be traded with ease."

Jim Rogers

Despite appearances, commodity futures contracts are not a recent innovation. The very first agricultural derivatives can be traced back to ancient Mesopotamia. There, King Hammurabi's legal code allowed farmers to sell their goods at a pre-agreed on price for a future delivery date, much like modern day futures contracts.[145] Today, many commodities are traded on futures exchanges. Buyers (agents in the market) can purchase commodities for their own physical needs (for example, an airplane manufacturer trying to buy enough aluminium for an upcoming order). Sellers can secure a price for their own product at the best possible value (such as a farmer intending to secure a price for his wheat once harvested). Finally, speculators can buy and sell commodity futures contracts based on their view as to where the price will be in the future.

In commodity markets, strange events are always happening (unpredictable weather patterns or geopolitical developments) and so volatility is quite normal. Both commodity producers and consumers face considerable risks in ensuring that the commodities they supply/demand are delivered at the right time and at the right price so that their profit margins are protected.

Commodity futures exchanges now make business considerably more efficient and less risky for both commodity producers and consumers. The first futures exchange market was the Dōjima Rice Exchange in Japan, established in the 1730s to meet the needs of samurai who, being paid in rice, needed a stable conversion to currency in the event of a bad harvest. The world's oldest commodity futures exchange with standardised exchange-traded futures contracts was the Chicago Board of Trade (CBOT), which began in 1864 with wheat, corn, cattle and pigs being widely traded.

Futures markets provide a means for trading the probabilities of where crude and wheat prices will be at certain points in the future, as derived from the real and ever-changing fundamental risks in the underlying physical markets. Participants in a futures market do not even have to take delivery of the commodities, a feature that is especially useful for speculators who can use the markets to take positions on the value of a particular commodity at various dates into the future. Moreover, regular contract expiries force a check of these assessments back to the condition of the underlying physical markets (see Chapter 43).[146]

The shape of this series of future prices is known as the futures curve. A futures curve is described as "in contango" when it is upward sloping and so prices in six months' time are higher than the spot price. This is also known as a normal curve or a normal market. In general, traders are willing to pay a premium to avoid the costs associated with transporting, storing and insuring a commodity (known as the cost to carry); therefore, the furthest-out contracts are typically higher in price. In contrast, when the shape of the futures price curve is downward sloping, the futures price of a commodity in say six months' time is lower than the current spot price, and so the market is said to be in backwardation. This is also known as an inverted curve or an inverted market. If a futures curve moves towards backwardation (also described as a tightening in the futures curve), it is a good sign that the current underlying conditions in a commodity market are getting tighter – either via gradually improving demand or supply problems, or a combination of both. The opposite of which is so when the curve moves towards contango.

The shape of the futures curve has significant implications for commodity producers, consumers and investors. In the event that a commodity futures curve is in backwardation, producers might choose to run down stocks or look to increase output, taking advantage of the tight market and fearing that they could get a lower price in the future. In contrast, if the futures curve is in contango, a producer may want to put the commodity into storage and sell it at a higher price in the future.

The difference between spot and futures prices for a commodity is known as the basis. The price of a futures contract – whether it is above or below the spot price – will converge to the spot price as the expiration date on the contract approaches. This process is called convergence. For someone holding a futures contract where the market is in backwardation, the value of their contract will rise to meet the spot price, enabling them to achieve what is known as a positive roll yield, ie, a bit of income from selling one futures contract and buying another. The opposite applies for a trader holding a futures contract where the market is in contango.

John Maynard Keynes' "normal backwardation" theory suggests that forward prices will always tend to be discounted to the market's expected future spot price in order to give investors an incentive to take on risk from producer hedgers. Which means even if the price is estimated correctly, the traded price will tend to under-state the market's real price forecast. Forward prices have been used extensively in the macroeconomic models used by central banks and other official agencies, and it is very tempting to view them as a price forecast. But even a cursory review of the forward curve's behaviour in recent years shows forward prices have been very poor predictors of realised spot commodity prices.[147]

The reason why futures are so poor at forecasting is because the forward curve shows the price at which it is possible to buy or sell futures contracts for a forward date at a price agreed on today. It is not a forecast of future spot prices (see Chapter 4 for why the forward curve may have some use in understanding the cost of production of a particular commodity).

As well as the cost of carry, the convenience yield and the influence of "normal backwardation theory", there are a number of other factors to be aware of which affect the forward curve – other than just market expectations of where the price of a commodity will be in the future. First, there is the physical characteristic of the commodity, eg, whether it is easy to store, whether there are ample inventories etc. Second, that imperfect market liquidity can substantially hinder anyone's ability to buy or sell at the price they believe prices may eventually end up. Third and finally, the curve fails to account for inflation.

One or another commodity index is often quoted in the press to state that commodity prices have reached this or that level. This is misleading, however. These indexes typically track the price of a basket of commodities, but also capture the roll yield (either positive or negative) from selling one futures contract near expiry and then buying another contract, ie, the impact of backwardation or contango. Furthermore, they generally only capture those commodities that are traded on futures exchanges, so they miss out on a number of significant commodities like steel, and many indexes involve frequent rebalancing, making it even more difficult to compare one period with another.

The essential thing:

Commodity futures exchanges make business considerably more efficient and less risky for both commodity producers and consumers.

*Want to know more? Visit my blog **Materials Risk** and get email updates and analysis on what's really happening in commodities and commodity markets.*

43) Physical commodity markets

"We cannot help but compare the current price strength to the myth of Sisyphus."

Tamas Varga, PVM oil brokerage

It's essential to make the distinction between the physical market for a commodity and the futures market. Physical (also known as cash or spot) market prices are determined by the supply and demand for the physical commodity. Here, traders (perhaps from one of the commodity trading firms described in Chapter 33) buy oil, for example, from the producer and sell it to the refiner, for immediate delivery. Physical buyers and sellers have a direct pulse on the market and may immediately feel when it is well supplied, or not.

Futures prices, on the other hand, are determined by the supply and demand for futures positions in a particular commodity. Futures markets provide a means for trading the probability of where commodity prices will be at certain points in the future, allowing physical market participants a means by which they can hedge their position and so reduce risk (see Chapter 31).

Historically, for agriculture at least, farmers would bring their produce (crops and livestock etc.) to a central marketplace where it could be sold off to buyers. Although this still happens on a small scale, the majority of physical commodities now normally trade in an Over-The-Counter (OTC) market. This market is not actually based anywhere physically. Instead, traders, buyers and sellers deal directly with each other over the telephone or through other means.

For many commodities, physical markets determined by the interaction of supply and demand are, perhaps surprisingly, a relatively new innovation. Take the most important commodity of all – oil. Prior to the early 1970s, only approximately 5% of the world's oil was freely traded, whereas the other 95% was determined by long-term contracts with fixed prices.[148] Meanwhile, up until 2003, iron ore prices were also based on long-term contracts between the largest iron ore miners and Japanese steelmakers. However, as China became an increasing presence in the iron ore market, the big miners abandoned long-term contracts and began to sell their ore on short-term contracts based on prices set on a nascent spot market (see Chapter 11 on ferrous metals).

Despite how it might appear though, most commodity prices are actually very difficult to find. It's easy, I hear you say, just look on the internet for the latest price for a barrel of Brent crude oil or a tonne of copper. However, the prices quoted in the newspaper or online tend to be for the nearest dated futures contract for a particular commodity, rather than the price at which actual buyers and sellers traded at in the spot market. In reality, the prices of most commodities actually used to produce stuff in the real world are merely estimates based on incomplete information in the physical OTC markets.

Commodity prices are generally discovered through a process of interpreting what sources (buyers and sellers) in a particular commodity market say on bids, offers and deals, whilst also accounting for other factors like shipping costs, the size of the deal that took place and a whole host of other factors. These prices are then published by price reporting agencies. With some industry estimates suggesting that as much as 80% of all crude and oil product transactions are linked to reference prices, their accuracy is therefore essential.[149]

In contrast to commodity futures markets where speculators try to anticipate future demand and supply and the likely effect on price, physical commodity markets are influenced by current fundamentals. Regular futures contract expiries should, in theory at least, mean that the physical and futures markets do not get too far out of line. Although the physical fundamentals of supply and demand prevail eventually, the physical market may not always be able to anchor futures prices for days, months or even years. It takes time for the market to divert and accumulate sufficient physical supplies from normal business channels to meet a rise in futures prices driven by speculative rather than fundamental factors. In the meantime, futures prices are more likely to drive the physical market, rather than the other way around. Putting it another way, the futures tail really can wag the physical dog.

Commodity trading firms act as essential intermediaries in physical commodity markets. Virtually all commodities must undergo a variety of processes in order to transform them into things that we can actually consume (see Chapter 30). These transformations can be grouped into space (commodities tend to be produced far from where they are actually needed), time (harvests happen once a year, but consumption occurs all year round) and form (they are refined in some way). Given their level of involvement in physical commodity markets, trading firms have their finger firmly on the pulse, able to detect changes in the underlying fundamentals affecting physical markets. Given this knowledge, many trading firms use it to make well-informed bets on the futures markets. Often they may even seek to lose money on a physical trade, in order to make more money on a commodity futures trade.

The essential thing:

Physical commodity markets are where buyers and sellers come together to trade commodities for immediate delivery.

44) Speculation and commodity markets

"How can we ignore the fact that food has become an object of speculation or is connected to movements in a financial market that, lacking in clear rules and moral principles, seems anchored on the sole objective of profit?"

Pope Benedict XVI

Commodities are an asset class in their own right. Financial innovation has meant that anyone can now take a stake in one or a basket of different commodities. Investment in the sector has been supported by the belief that investor portfolios could benefit from the diversification that commodities could bring.

The type of participants in commodity markets has changed since 2000. As well as commercial firms (farmers, manufacturers and consumers etc.) and non-commercial firms (such as hedge funds), there has been a large inflow of investment capital from commodity index investors (CITs). CITs seek exposure to commodities as part of a broader portfolio strategy, often investing in instruments linked to broad based indices, like the Goldman Sachs Commodity Index. This large inflow of capital into commodity markets since 2000 has generated heated debate about whether this "financialisation" has distorted commodity prices, perhaps resulting in consumers paying higher prices than underlying fundamentals would suggest.

Hedge fund manager Michael W. Masters has led the charge against investor interest in food prices, arguing that unprecedented buying pressure from new financial index investors has created a massive bubble in agricultural commodities at various times in recent years.[150] However, other studies have found little evidence to support this. This is not to say that the large influx of index investment did not have any impact in agricultural futures markets. There is some evidence that index investment may have resulted in a very slight upward pressure on futures prices before contracts expire and also contributed to a small narrowing of price spreads during the period when index investors roll trades across futures contracts.[151]

It is essential to understand that investors in index products are also regular sellers of futures, because they must routinely roll their positions as contract expiries near. Moreover, because they often target certain dollar exposures as a share of their total portfolio – as prices rise, the index investors' demand for futures falls and they buy less during roll periods. Conversely, when prices fall, the portfolio weights also fall below target and the index investor will buy more to offset the shortfall. In this way, it can be argued that the index investor adds to the overall stability of the market, because he is a net seller when the market calls for supply and a net buyer when the market calls for demand.

In contrast to the passive commodity index investors, more active speculators have a much more prominent role to play in price discovery. Speculators who expect wheat to be in short supply and see wheat prices rising in the future can back their hunches by purchasing wheat futures contracts on a commodity futures exchange. Wheat futures contracts represent claims to wheat to be delivered at a specified price and at a specified date and place in the future. But remember, buying a futures contract for wheat does not reduce the quantity of wheat that is available for consumption. If many speculators share the view that shortages will worsen and prices will rise, then their demand for wheat futures will be high and, consequently, the price of wheat for future delivery will also rise. This then provides the incentive for farmers to plant more wheat and/or increase yields to serve this demand, helping to alleviate future shortages.

Speculators also perform a much needed service for physical traders. Commercial sellers, such as farmers intending to hedge next season's crop, tend to be on the short side of the futures market, ie, they are intending to sell. Financial investors (in particular CIT's) tend to be on the long side of the futures market, ie, they are intending to buy.

Commercial buyers, however, are less likely to hedge. In contrast to commercial sellers who face concentrated price risk in the commodity that they produce, commercial consumers tend to face price risks across multiple commodities and so the cost of trading deters them from hedging risk. As such, speculators provide a much needed source of liquidity, while reducing the discount that commercial sellers might otherwise need to offer to get a buyer.

The debate about speculators, futures markets and commodity prices is nothing new. The humble onion holds significant lessons. Back in 1957, a group of traders and farmers in the US cornered the onion market and sent the onion futures price rocketing. The onion price eventually plummeted and pressure grew from those who had lost money in the boom for futures trading in onions to be banned. The ban is still in force today. However, numerous studies have found that volatility actually rose after the ban was introduced.

The same bulbous root has also brought tears to people's eyes in India, because of high and volatile prices. Again, as in the US, the introduction of a futures market that could dampen volatility is seen as too politically sensitive. The lesson from the example of the onion is that like other commodities it is easy to blame the anonymous, invisible speculator, rather than addressing the fundamental reason for why a market may be failing.[152]

The financialisation of commodities is happening in other ways too. Commodities are also increasingly used as collateral or security for a loan, so failure to pay results in the lender selling the commodity. In order for a commodity to act as collateral it should be as cheap as possible to store and, as importantly, should not degrade over time. In the early days, the "commodity" could have been anything: wine, grain, livestock, metal, precious stones etc. These days, such collateral is much more likely to be something with a high value-to-density ratio, such as gold, silver or nickel (note that despite being bulkier and perishable, agricultural commodities like soybeans and natural rubber are increasingly playing a similar role).

The use of commodities as collateral has been particularly popular in China for cash strapped companies unable to secure credit using traditional banking channels. Various estimates suggest that approximately one-third of copper imported into China may have been passing through financing deals.[153]

The essential thing:

Commodity markets and speculators have always had an uncomfortable relationship.

45) Commodity market manipulation

"In the final analysis, it doesn't matter what you crazy people in California do, because I got smart guys who can always figure out how to make money."

Kenneth Lay, Enron CEO

"The word 'manipulation'... in its use is so broad as to include any operation in the cotton market that does not suit the gentleman who is speaking at the moment."

William Clayton, cotton broker

Commodity futures markets serve two crucial functions, both of which can become compromised if markets are being manipulated. The first function is facilitating the efficient transfer of risk from the risk averse to the risk tolerant. Firms or individuals that want to "hedge" against the risk of price movements can essentially lock in a price at which they can buy or sell in the future by trading on the futures market. Individuals or firms that are willing to bear price risk at low cost – usually referred to as speculators – take the other side of a hedgers' trades.[154]

The second function of futures markets is to transmit valuable information about supply and demand conditions. Individuals with a view about these fundamentals can buy or sell if it implies that the futures price is too low or too high. This "price discovery" function is valuable because producers, consumers and storers of the commodity can use the information embedded in futures prices to make better resource allocation decisions.

Manipulation is condemned because it interferes with these two essential functions of commodity futures markets. But what exactly constitutes a commodity market manipulation? The most direct strategy is to simply buy up a large percentage of the available commodity offered for sale in some spot market and hoard it. With the advent of futures trading, the party attempting to corner the market may then buy a large number of futures contracts on the commodity and then sell them at a profit after inflating the price.

Detailed throughout history, there have been many accounts of attempts to corner markets in everything from tin to cattle. However, to date, very few have ever succeeded (at least those that we know about!). The party attempting to corner a market can become very vulnerable because of the size of their position, especially if their attempt to corner the market becomes widely known. If the rest of the market senses weakness, it may resist any attempt to drive the market artificially any further by actively taking opposing positions. When the price starts to move against the "cornerer", they are in a very difficult position because it can become impossible to exit their position without catastrophically moving prices against themselves. In such a situation, traders on the other side of the trade may be able to profit from the cornerer's need to unwind their position.

The markets, especially for many agricultural commodities, are relatively small compared to the amount of money that can be amassed by hedge funds and other financial operators. In addition, markets may be very sensitive to perceived or actual threats to supply, especially if supply is concentrated on one significant exporter. Markets can also be opaque, meaning that it can be very difficult to find information on current production, quality or whether output is threatened by civil unrest. Having access to this kind of information, or indeed just being able to take advantage of a period of uncertainty, may allow a speculator to corner a market.[155]

In July 2010, Armajaro, a London-based commodity hedge fund, tried to corner the cocoa market, accumulating 24,100 cocoa futures contracts (a single "contract" is equal to ten metric tons of cocoa beans). The Armajaro cocoa stash was enormous, enough to fill five dry-bulk carriers the size of the Titanic or to make 12 billion 50g chocolate bars. In fact, 241,000 tons of cocoa was equivalent to the entire supply of cocoa in Europe, equal to 7% of annual global production and would have been worth close to US $1 billion at the going price of cocoa at the time. On this occasion, however, the market reacted predictably by driving cocoa prices to their highest levels in over four decades, only to have prices slide back down a few months later on the strength of a bumper cocoa crop in the Ivory Coast. In the end, Armajaro lost money on the bet, in part because of warehousing and storage costs running into as much as $10 million a month.

In 2000/01, energy supplier Enron manipulated electricity prices in California by taking advantage of the commoditisation of electricity and the complex rules behind the deregulation of the industry in the state. This market manipulation, combined with the effects of drought and delays in approving new power plants, led to an electricity supply shortage that caused wholesale electricity prices to rise by 800% between April and December 2000. Enron and others were able to manipulate their electricity production to take advantage of the rules and the market uncertainty. Manipulation strategies were known to energy traders under names such as "Fat Boy", "Death Star", "Forney Perpetual Loop", "Ricochet", "Ping Pong", "Black Widow", "Big Foot", "Red Congo", "Cong Catcher" and "Get Shorty".[156] [157]

Although you might think that the price of all commodities are easy to find, the price of Brent or WTI crude oil are quoted in the newspaper, for example. In reality, the prices of most commodities are merely estimates based on incomplete information from unregulated and illiquid markets. Commodity prices are generally discovered through a process of interpreting what sources in the market say on bids, offers and deals, while also accounting for other factors like shipping costs, the size of the deal that took place and a whole host of other factors. The accuracy of these commodity prices are essential, with some estimates suggesting that as much as 80% of all crude and oil product transactions are linked to reference prices (see Chapter 43).

Given the importance of these commodities to the working of the real economy, it is perhaps no surprise that any suspicion that prices have been manipulated (either by cornering a market or supplying misleading commodity price data) gathers a lot of attention from the authorities. Commodity market manipulation can impose substantial deadweight costs on futures markets and their users. Commodities ranging from gas and oil to gold and silver have been the centre of investigations by both US and European authorities since the early 2000s.

Regulation that reduces the frequency and impact of corners may well improve the efficiency of these markets. One proposal often raised is position limits, a cap on the amount of futures contracts that any individual can hold, thereby limiting the potential for manipulation. Sounds good in practice, right? But by restricting large traders, those most knowledgeable about the market and most able to bear risk, markets are less able to perform their essential tasks of transferring risk and transmitting valuable information.

The essential thing:

Commodity markets are vulnerable to manipulation.

*Want to know more? Visit my blog **Materials Risk** and get email updates and analysis on what's really happening in commodities and commodity markets.*

46) The arguments for and against investing in commodities

"Think big, think positive, never show any sign of weakness. Always go for the throat. Buy low, sell high. Fear? That's the other guy's problem. Nothing you have ever experienced will prepare you for the absolute carnage you are about to witness. Super Bowl, World Series – they don't know what pressure is. In this building, it's either kill or be killed. You make no friends in the pits and you take no prisoners. One minute you're up half a million in soybeans and the next, boom, your kids don't go to college and they've repossessed your Bentley. Are you with me?"

Louis Winthorpe III (aka Dan Aykroyd), Trading Places

The film *Trading Places* perhaps typified how investing and trading in commodities was perceived in the early 2000s – a very risky place to be and certainly not, as the saying goes, for widows and orphans. However, the author and investor Jim Rogers was one of many that helped change the negative investor attitude that surrounded the inclusion of commodities in an investment portfolio. Of course, as with all investments, if you go in too deep, you risk losing your shirt, but, as Rogers explains, it would be foolish to ignore the benefits of such an important asset.

Stop right there! Before you jump straight into the how, let's have a look at the argument for investing in commodities. Although it is an important asset (otherwise why would I write a book about them in the first place?), don't expect to make a lot of money by investing in commodities over the long term. Commodity returns can be separated into the "price" return (ie, a change in the underlying price for one or a basket of commodities) and the "income" return (ie, the roll yield from selling a futures contract before expiry and purchasing a new contract at a discount, plus the risk premium for taking on risk from producers hedges). If you jumped straight to this chapter, it's worth reading Chapter 42 first because it's not obvious that either type of return is a dependable source of compoundable profit.

As we saw in Chapter 7, bull markets in commodities tend to end where they start. Indeed, evidence suggests their expected long-run real return (ie, after inflation) is essentially zero. If you look at *The Economist*'s commodity-price index from 1871 through to the end of 2010, it is up a measly 50% – an annual real return of 0.003%![158] To understand why, consider how commodity prices influence the price of end products and services. When a company uses a commodity such as aluminium to build a car, the cost of that aluminium is listed as part of the expense. If for some reason the cost of aluminium goes up, the car manufacturer will have to increase the price of the car in order to make a profit in excess of the cost of production. In other words, the price of cars will rise because the price of aluminium has risen (all else being equal). For this reason, commodities tend to correlate closely with the rate of inflation because they represent a large portion of the costs that producers try to pass on to their end buyers.

The second factor that forms part of a commodity investor's return is the "income" return. The first part, the roll yield is where current futures contracts are rolled into new futures contracts upon expiry, in order to capture the lower price. As we see in Chapter 42, this requires a market to be in backwardation. Yet, over the past ten years or so, commodity futures markets have tended towards contango, resulting in a negative roll yield for investors. The second part is the risk premium and this arises because forward prices will always tend to be discounted to the market's expected future spot price in order to give investors a "risk premium" to take on risk from producer hedgers (known as "normal backwardation" theory). This means that even if the price is estimated correctly, the traded futures price will tend to understate the market's real price forecast. The risk premium in commodities was thought to be about equal to that in stocks and better than the premium in bonds.[159] Even though commodities doubled between 2003 and 2014, any investors who assigned money to commodity Goldman Sachs Commodity Index (GSCI) products in that period on a total return basis may be sitting on zero returns.[160]

One of the proposed benefits of including commodities in a portfolio was that they were uncorrelated with other asset prices (like equities and bonds, for example). This offered the prospect that commodities could continue to offer some return, even if equity markets turned down, while also being an alternative hedge against risks like inflation. The correlation between commodity and other asset price changes was near 20% in the 1980s and 1990s, but by 2013 however the correlation was closer to 60% (see Chapter 44 on the financialisation of commodity markets to see why that happened), although that has since dropped again.[161]

Remember, when you buy commodities as an investment, you're selling human ingenuity. A bushel of wheat, a lump of coal or an ingot of silver today is identical with a bushel of wheat, a lump of coal or an ingot of silver produced 140 or more years ago (see Chapter 35 on technology and innovation). Investing directly in oil or mining companies is another way of gaining exposure to one or a basket of different commodities, while also capturing the added value from human ingenuity. In contrast to investing directly in a particular commodity resource, company shares typically pay a dividend.

Note that share prices are not always correlated with the price of the underlying commodity. Factors such as capital expenditure, government policies (see Chapter 27 on resource nationalism), management, balance sheet and accounting practices, unforeseen operational issues (a miners' strike, for example) and the general appetite amongst investors can all affect the share price. The demand for commodities and the ability for supply to respond can be highly cyclical, and this can also be reflected in the share price for resource companies.

As Jim Rogers explains, the value of a commodity will never approach zero, something that could happen with a company. In contrast to a company, however, a commodity provides no income stream, and as other chapters of this book illustrate its value can be subject to wild swings if there is a shock to either demand or supply. That's not to say that commodities don't offer potential. Commodities can offer the potential for substantial gains on a tactical short-term basis, just not as a long-term investment. If after this disclaimer you are undaunted, Chapter 47 includes a review of some of the ways you can access commodities, either as a long-term investment or as a short-term trading strategy.

The essential thing:

Don't mistake the fruits of production for the
means of production.

47) How to trade or invest in commodity markets

"The problem with commodities is that you are betting on what someone else would pay for them in six months. The commodity itself isn't going to do anything for you… it is an entirely different game to buy a lump of something and hope that somebody else pays you more for that lump two years from now than it is to buy something that you expect to produce income for you over time."

Warren Buffet

"Stock prices can go to zero. Commodities cannot. Unlike shares in a company commodities are real things that are always likely to be worth something to somebody."

Jim Rogers

One option is to actually buy and hold the commodity itself. Historically, many people have sought to hold a commodity in physical form, either as an investment or as a store of value. The commodity that has traditionally held this role has been gold, but also other precious metals like silver. Holding a commodity in physical form has its downsides though, its security namely, but also the lack of a ready market to sell it in the event that you want your money back. Nowadays, the purchase of precious metals tends to be on deposit at a bank so that they can store it on your behalf, for a charge of course.

For direct exposure to commodity prices, investors generally buy exchange-traded products (ETPs). Physical ETPs usually provide exposure to the price of a commodity and are "backed" by the equivalent value of the actual product, stored securely in a vault. Physical ETPs tend to only feature precious metals such as gold and silver. Futures-based ETPs meanwhile use futures or swap contracts to provide exposure without any physical holdings. The difference between the two attributed to counter party risk. Critics of futures-based funds argue that counter party risk is higher, since these funds only hold paper promising the delivery of a commodity, exposing investors to the risk of non-payment.

Investors' returns may also be adversely affected when the ETP manager sells expiring futures contracts and replaces them with longer-dated ones at a higher price (a situation common in commodity markets known as contango). However, when near term prices are higher than future ones (a condition known as backwardation), the ETP investor gains when the positions are rolled over (see Chapter 42).

Commodity index funds, in contrast, involve buying or selling futures to replicate the performance of the index or sometimes entering into swaps with investment banks who themselves then trade the futures. Bear in mind though that the weighting afforded to different commodities within a given index may have a significant bearing on the risk and the potential return of investing in an index fund.

Investing directly in companies involved with energy, mining or agriculture is another way of gaining exposure to one or a basket of different commodities. As explained in Chapter 46, the share price for an individual mining company may diverge significantly from the price of the metal that it extracts. One way investors can look to reduce this risk is to invest in a fund that includes a number of companies operating in a particular sector. Other funds invest in companies (such as food and drink manufacturers) that take virgin commodities and turn them into the end products that you and I consume. In this example, higher agricultural prices may hurt returns as manufacturing costs increase.

In contrast to ETPs and shares, spread betting and contract for differences (CFDs) offer a way for investors to bet on the direction of particular commodities, either up or down. A CFD is a contract between two parties whereby the seller will pay the buyer the difference between the current value of an asset and its value at some future time (if the difference is negative, then the buyer pays to the seller instead). Traders in CFDs are required to maintain a certain amount of margin (usually ranging from 0.5% to 30%). One advantage of not having to put up the full amount of the CFD as collateral is that a given quantity of capital can control a larger position, amplifying the potential for profit or loss. Note that you cannot take physical delivery of the commodity using CFDs!

As an example, if you think US crude (WTI) is going to rise, you might open a long position by buying 100 barrels of US crude CFDs at $61.04 per barrel. The value of the opening trade is $6,104 and as the margin requirement is 1% therefore the amount required to be paid by the buyer upfront is $61.04. The price subsequently rises to $62.64 and the position is closed by selling 100 barrels at $62.64, therefore generating a return of $1.60 per barrel, or a total profit of $160.

So how does a spread bet work? Say you take the view that the price of cocoa is going to rise because of civil unrest in West Africa, the spread betting company might quote a price of $2,950-$2,955 per tonne in the daily futures market (the bid price on the left being the price you can sell at and the offer price, on the right side being the price you can buy at). You decide to bet $10 a point (in this example each $1 is a point) at $2,955 in the expectation that prices will go up. The price quickly rises to $3,020-$3,025 per tonne and you sell at £3,020 per tonne, netting $650 (65 points x $10).[162]

Spread betting companies typically offer prices for a range of commodities, including copper, cocoa, oil and natural gas. Getting exposure to commodities through spread betting goes back a long way. The origins of the IG (Investors Gold) Index reflect this. IG was founded on the back of traders' wish for an easy way to punt on the gold price back in the 1970s.

There are serious risks involved with CFDs and spread betting because the contract is two-way. Just as the spread betting provider will pay you if you call the commodity price movement correctly, so you will have to pay out if you get it wrong. And just as the borrowing involved magnifies your profits, so it also magnifies losses.

The essential thing:

There are several ways for investors and traders to gain exposure to commodity markets, but, as with all assets, be aware of the risks (and the marketing spin) before jumping in.

*Want to know more? Visit my blog **Materials Risk** and get email updates and analysis on what's really happening in commodities and commodity markets.*

48) Technical analysis, seasonality and noise

"If something cannot go on forever, it will stop."

Herbert Stein

"Fundamentalists that don't pay attention to the charts are like a doctor who says he's not going to take a patient's temperature."

Bruce Kovner

Most of the 50 things in this book focus on what is commonly known as fundamental analysis – demand, supply, stocks, costs and everything in between. Many traders (but also physical buyers and sellers of commodities) also focus on technical analysis. In short, technical analysis involves analysing past price patterns, trends and volume in order to try and determine future price movements.

The most popular indicators for commodity trading fall under the category of momentum indicators, which follow the trusted adage for all traders, "buy low and sell high". These indicators are further split into oscillators and trend following indicators. Traders need to first identify the market – ie, whether the market is trending or ranging – before applying any of these indicators. This is important because the trend following indicators do not perform well in a ranging market; similarly, oscillators tend to be misleading in a trending market.[163]

One of the simplest and most widely used indicators in technical analysis is the moving average (MA), which is the average price for a commodity over a specified period. For example, a 200-day MA will be the average of the closing prices over the last 200 days, including the current period. The crossover by a short term MA above a longer term MA is suggestive of an upswing.

The Relative Strength Index (RSI) is a popular and easy to apply technical momentum indicator. It attempts to determine the overbought and oversold level in a market on a scale of 0 to 100, thus indicating if the market has topped or bottomed. According to this indicator, the markets are considered overbought above 70 and oversold below 30.

The Bollinger Band is also thought to be a good indicator of overbought and oversold conditions in a commodity market. The Bollinger Bands are a set of three lines: the centre line (trend) with an upper line (resistance) and a lower line (support). When the price of the commodity considered is volatile, the bands tend to expand, but when the prices are range bound there is contraction. Bollinger Bands are helpful in detecting the turning points in a range bound market – buying when the price drops and hits the lower band and selling when prices rise to touch the upper band.

Yet there are some big question marks around technical analysis. The flaw in technical trading is best described by the random walk hypothesis, a theory developed by Eugene Fama. This theory says that the past movement of any financial asset (be it stocks or commodities) are of absolutely no help in predicting future movements. We all know that even if a coin comes up heads ten times in a row, the probability of heads on the next throw is still fifty-fifty. Likewise, the random walk hypothesis says that even if a commodity price has risen for the last ten days, it tells you nothing about what it will do tomorrow.

Seasonal trends are thought by many to give an indication of where prices may move next. Talk of a consistent seasonal pattern in the price of any financial asset should always be viewed with suspicion. Seasonal tendencies are just that - tendencies. The existence of such a pattern (at least where the price swing is substantial) would imply that the market is so inefficient that some participants would be able to profit at the expense of others simply by following the calendar.

Let's take gold as an example. First, the seasonal drivers of the demand for gold are hardly a secret. Sales of gold (especially jewellery) pick up in the autumn and winter because of the timing of harvests, the Indian wedding season and festivals associated with gift-giving (Diwali, Thanksgiving and Christmas). Every year there is the flurry of stories about the impact this may have on the price of gold. Hence, there cannot be many market participants who are not aware of this.

Second, the physical characteristics that make gold a popular store of value also make it easier to hold stocks to arbitrage away any seasonal price patterns. Above all, gold is durable (not like foodstuffs) and it has a high value-to-volume ratio (in contrast to oil). Meanwhile, there is also a large amount of old (scrap) gold that can come back on to the market. Gold is fungible in the sense that because of its high durability refined gold is considered identical with scrap gold.[164]

Like other markets, unless you are actively trading a particular commodity on a frequent (daily) basis you should be wary of paying too much attention to the deluge of minute by minute analysis that is available. It can be incredibly tempting to see signals in what is really just noise. A lot of journalists and commentators are paid to write stories explaining the reason why a particular commodity did this or that on one particular day.

Remember a commodity market is not only made up of speculators. There are actual physical buyers and sellers who are trying to trade their produce or hedge their purchasing risk. As we saw in Chapter 43, it is dangerous for physical traders to get too involved in trying to time the market. Meanwhile, as we saw with Doctor Copper in Chapter 12, it is dangerous to place too much emphasis on one indicator, whether that is a commodity price or something else. There are just too many other factors at work.

The essential thing:

Technical analysis involves analysing historical price patterns, trends and volume to try and predict future price movements.

49) Market psychology

"What the wise man does in the beginning, the fool does in the end."

Warren Buffet

In theory, commodity markets should at least act to reflect the opinions of buyers and sellers regarding demand, supply and the future direction of the price. However, they are also influenced by the emotions and perceptions of risk of those who trade them, including producers, consumers, traders and investors.

But first, ask yourself this. What exactly is the right price for a commodity?

You might say it lies where demand and supply intersect (the equilibrium price) and the market is balanced. But, as we know from other chapters in this book, commodity markets are rarely in equilibrium.

If you look at a company, a property or another asset that produces an income stream, you can use the price/earnings ratio, yields and capitalisation rates to give a good idea of what the value should be. But how do you value a non-income producing asset like a commodity? Take oil as an example. You can say that supply is finite, that it will run out soon and that much of it is in the hands of nations that we can't rely on, but what does that make it worth?

The same factors were just as relevant when oil was approximately $40 per barrel in December 2008 as they were in July 2007 when oil reached $147 per barrel. In the end, the commodity is only worth what someone is prepared to pay for it. People's perception of scarcity in July 2007 meant they were willing to pay over three times what they would pay just a year and a half later. This leads us on to how efficient commodity markets are at incorporating information.

The Efficient Market Hypothesis (EMH) essentially says that at any one time, asset prices (including commodity markets) already reflect everything we know. From the point of view of commodity markets, this would mean that there is no point (from an investment or procurement point of view) in trying to time the market, no point in researching the underlying fundamentals of a commodity, no point in even watching the news or the latest commodity price nor indeed any point in reading blogs like MATERIALS RISK.[165]

Some commodity markets are evidently more efficient than others at incorporating new fundamental information. Researchers from the Academy of Sciences and Charles University in the Czech Republic analysed the market efficiency of 25 commodity futures across various groups – metals, energy, softs, grains and other agricultural commodities. They found that energy commodities (heating oil and crude) are among the most efficient commodities, while other agricultural commodities (primarily livestock) are the least efficient.[166] Intuitively this would seem to make sense. Energy markets are much more transparent, both in terms of data availability and the factors that affect consumption, for example temperature. Markets like livestock are much more opaque. An insight into current and potential future supply (possibly only the farmer who knows) might give a buyer/trader an advantage over other market participants. From an investor's point of view, one wanting to find where hard work and skill could see the biggest pay off, an understanding of which commodities are least efficient could be essential.

Commodity markets are different from other assets. Demand for equities tends to rise as share prices increase and as investors flock to a particular share or market in anticipation of further price increases. As commodity prices rise, demand for commodities tends to decrease as users reduce their consumption and look for alternatives, while supply tends to increase as producers look to take advantage of higher demand and price levels. However, market participants can make perverse decisions if they don't appreciate this. When seeing a snapshot of commodity prices in isolation, ie, the first decade or so of the 2000s, people understandably conclude that prices can only ever go in one direction, a sort of commodity.com. As we saw in Chapter 7 on commodity super-cycles, emotions (euphoria or despair) will be everywhere at both the top and the bottom of the market.

The essential thing:

The price of a commodity is ultimately worth what someone is prepared to pay for it and that, in turn, is determined by their perception of scarcity.

50) Don't begin an argument with the price

"What 'everyone knows' is usually unhelpful at best and wrong at worst."

Howard Marks

"High oil prices set to tip world into recession." This headline is a prime example of just looking at the price and making a conclusion about the impact. Yet without looking at what is actually causing the price movement, it can be unclear what the actual consequences will be. Many market participants tend to concentrate too narrowly on the impact that a change in a commodity price will have. Yet this can create misleading logic and outcomes akin to the phrase "the tail wagging the dog". Don't begin an argument with the price, instead focus on the fundamentals.

The collapse in the price of oil from mid-2014 is also telling. Many traders had been so accustomed to demand related oil shocks that many misinterpreted what it would mean for the eventual recovery in the price of oil. Previous sharp falls in the price of oil, because of changes in demand, have tended to be followed relatively swiftly by a rebound in prices. A kind of "V" shaped recovery. However, this particular drop in oil prices could be characterised as a positive supply shock. Previous incarnations of which have exhibited a "U" or a "W" shaped recovery in prices.

Let's look at another headline, this time from 2009: "Sharks off the British coast: Oil tankers refuse to unload until prices rise... keeping YOUR fuel costs soaring."[167] At the time, the oil market was in contango – where near term prices are lower than those further out. Prices do not cause fundamental shifts, but rather reflect fundamental shifts. On this occasion, a market surplus forced a build-up in inventories, which in turn generated the contango. The nasty sharks off the British coast (ie, the oil traders) were storing oil in tankers because the market structure allowed them to, the structure of which is reflective of there being a glut of supply on the market.

It's important to always go at least one step forward in understanding the impact of a change in market fundamentals. Many people suffer from a failure of imagination, where they can easily grasp the immediate impact of a development, but fail to understand the second, third and fourth order consequences. You may understand this more by the word "contagion". The term is often used to express how what appear to be small changes ripple out affecting markets with apparently unconnected consequences.

So what is the impact of lower oil prices? Well, it could mean lower revenue for oil producing nations like Saudi Arabia. But what would that mean? It could result in them pulling money back that they have invested elsewhere in the world (the US, in particular) to help prop up their budgets. The repatriation of these so-called "Petrodollars" may then lead to a decline in the value of the US dollar. But what about a long-term impact? Oil producing nations seeing the risk of permanently lower oil prices might then invest in other means of producing energy that has a higher long term return. Solar power anyone?

To take another example, what was the impact of a severe drought in Brazil ahead of a football tournament? Well, although it would be natural to assume that supplies of sugar, coffee and soybeans are likely to be negatively impacted, it's not so obvious that it would lead to the country importing high cost LNG. Brazil typically meets 70% of its electricity demand from hydroelectric sources. Ahead of the Football World Cup in 2014, the Brazilian government, keen to avoid draining its scant water resources any more than it needed to, resorted to importing significant volumes of LNG instead, to avoid the lights going out.[168]

The essential thing:

Don't begin an argument with the price, instead focus on the fundamentals; always look for the second, third and fourth order impacts.

Congratulations you've finished the book. I would very much appreciate it if you could leave a review. They really do make a big difference.

Want to know more? Visit my blog **Materials Risk** *and get email updates and analysis on what's really happening in commodities and commodity markets.*

[1] Commodity, by Wikipedia contributors. (ND). *Wikipedia*. **https://en.wikipedia.org/wiki/Commodity**.

[2] Commodity Markets Outlook, by the World Bank Group. (October 2014). *Global Economic Prospects*. **http://www.worldbank.org/content/dam/Worldbank/GEP/GEPcommodities/commodity_markets_outlook_2014_october.pdf**.

[3] UN FAO. **www.fao.org**.

[4] Fundamentals or Fads? Pipes, Not Punting, Explain Commodity Prices and Volatility, by Colin Fenton and Jonah Waxman. (2001). *J.P. Morgan Global Commodities Research Commodity Markets Outlook and Strategy*. **http://papers.ssrn.com/sol3/papers.cfm?abstract_id=1922759**.

[5] Note that the use of futures and other tools to hedge against a fall in commodity prices and ongoing service and delivery contracts may also delay a supply response.

[6] Commodity Prices and Volatility: Old Answers to New Questions, by Goldman Sachs. (2010) *Global Investment Research*. **http://www.goldmansachs.com/gsam/ch/advisors/en/ideas/global-economic-outlook/articles/Commodity-Prices-and-Volatility-Old-Answers-to-New-Questions.html**.

[7] Energy for Growing and Harvesting Crops is a Large Component of Farm Operating Costs, by Susan Hicks. (2014). *Today in Energy*. EIA. **http://www.eia.gov/todayinenergy/detail.cfm?id=18431**.

[8] Effects of Speculation and Interest Rates in a "Carry Trade" Model of Commodity Prices, by

Jeffery A. Frankel. (2013). *HKS Faculty Research Working Paper Series RWP13-022.* **https://research.hks.harvard.edu/publications/workingpapers/citation.aspx?PubId=9031&type=WPN.**

[9] The Economics of Exhaustible Resources, by Harold Hotelling. (1931). *The Journal of Political Economy.* 39(2): 137-175. **http://links.jstor.org/sici?sici=0022-3808%28193104%2939%3A2%3C137%3ATEOER%3E2.0.CO%3B2-G.**

[10] The Atlantic hurricane season stretches from June until November, although the most active stage tends to be between August 20th and the end of October.

[11] Why India's Monsoon is Raising the Pressure on Investors by Neena Rai and Debiprasad Nayak. (June 20th 2014). *The Wall Street Journal* **http://blogs.wsj.com/briefly/2014/06/20/why-indias-monsoon-is-raising-the-pressure-on-investors-the-short-answer/**

[12] "Breakout Nations: In Pursuit of the Next Economic Miracles", by Ruchir Sharma. (2013). Penguin

[13] "Hot Commodities: How Anyone Can Invest Profitably in the World's Best Market", by Jim Rogers. (2004). Random House Publishing Group, p. 5.

[14] Note that even in long periods of rising or falling commodity prices there may be periods where prices go against trend for long periods. Prices don't move in straight lines.

[15] Commodities and the Global Economy: Are Current Prices the New Normal?, by Paul Bloxham, Andrew Keen and Luke Hartigan. (August 2012). *HSBC.*

https://www.research.hsbc.com/midas/Res/RDV?p=
pdf&$sessionid$=GkRxhk5U2g4crjwqhtYaInw&key=U2
3WPWM8B0&n=338157.PDF.

[16] Popular Delusions: Commodities for the Long
Run? Not on Your Nellie – I'd Rather Eat
Coal!!, by Dylan Grice. (2010). *Societe
Generale*.
http://www.harringtoncooper.com/content/file/s
ocgen%20-
%20zero%20return%20on%20commodities_1382697846
.pdf.

[17] The Cobweb Theorem, by Mordecai Ezekiel.
(1938). *The Quarterly Journal of Economics*.
52(2): 255-280.
http://www.econ-
pol.unisi.it/paolopin/TeachMaterial/IntroMatla
bStata/Ezekiel1938.pdf.

[18] Rational Expectations and the Theory of
Price Movements, by John F. Muth. (1961).
*Econometrica: Journal of the Econometric
Society*. 29(3): 315-335.
www.fep.up.pt/docentes/pcosme/S-E-
1/se1_trab_0910/se1.pdf.

[19] "The General Theory of Employment, Interest
and Money", by John Maynard Keynes. (1936).
http://cas.umkc.edu/economics/people/facultypa
ges/kregel/courses/econ645/winter2011/generalt
heory.pdf.

[20] Why oil prices are so unstable, by John
Kemp. (December 12th 2014). *Reuters*.
http://www.reuters.com/article/2014/12/12/oil-
prices-cycles-kemp-idUSL6N0TW1RN20141212

[21] Oil Comes From Dinosaurs – Fact or Fiction?,
by Anne Marie Helmenstine. (ND). *about
education*.
http://chemistry.about.com/b/2014/05/07/oil-
comes-from-dinosaurs-fact-or-fiction.htm.

[22] How Oil Prices Translate To The Petrol Pump, by Ursula Errington. (January 30th 2013). *Sky News*. **http://news.sky.com/story/1045301/how-oil-prices-translate-to-the-petrol-pump**

[23] "The Solar Revolution" by Steve McKevitt and Tony Ryan. (2014). Icon Books Ltd.

[24] Biomass, by Wikipedia contributors. (ND). *Wikipedia*. **https://en.wikipedia.org/wiki/Biomass**.

[25] Geothermal energy, by Wikipedia contributors. (ND). *Wikipedia*. **https://en.wikipedia.org/wiki/Geothermal_energy**.

[26] Fukushima nuclear power site leaks 300 tons of radioactive water, by Dorothy Davis. (August 20th 2013). Penn Energy.

[27] Case Study of a Growth Driver – Silver Use in Solar, by Chris Berry. (July 21st 2014). *PVTECH*. **http://www.pv-tech.org/guest_blog/case_study_of_a_growth_driver_silver_use_in_solar**.

[28] Steel is an alloy based primarily on iron. As iron occurs only as iron oxides in the earth's crust, the ores must be converted, or "reduced", using carbon. The primary source of this carbon is coking coal.

[29] The Lore of Ore. (October 13th 2012). *The Economist*. **http://www.economist.com/node/21564559**

[30] The basics of iron ore, by Annie Gilroy. (July 16th 2014). *Market Realist*. **http://marketrealist.com/2014/07/must-know-basics-iron-ore/**

[31] Morgan Stanley Sees China Peak Steel Now as Goldman Differs, by Jasmine Ng. (February 2nd 2015). *Bloomberg Business*. **http://www.bloomberg.com/news/articles/2015-**

02-02/peak-steel-arrives-in-china-this-year-morgan-stanley-predicts.

[32] "World Steel in Figures 2014", by the World Steel Association. (2014).
http://www.worldsteel.org/dms/internetDocument List/bookshop/World-Steel-in-Figures-2014/document/World%20Steel%20in%20Figures%202014%20Final.pdf.

[33] Closing the Loop on Steel: What We Can Learn From a Manufacturer in Ecuador, by Wayne Visser. (November 20th 2014). *The Guardian*.
http://www.theguardian.com/sustainable-business/2014/nov/20/steel-recycling-circualr-economy-manufacturer-ecuador-adelca.

[34] Aluminium used to be much rarer. Back in the 1850s, it was considered a precious metal and was twice the price of gold (see Chapter 17 on gold and other precious metals).

[35] Bayer Process, by Wikipedia contributors. (ND). *Wikipedia*.
http://en.wikipedia.org/wiki/Bayer_process.

[36] Copper price as an economic indicator, by Casper Burgering. (October 2014). ABN Amro
https://www.abnamromarkets.com/fileadmin/user_upload/TA/2014/Economy-and-copperprice.pdf

[37] Global Economic View. Gold: A Six Thousand Year-old Bubble Revisited, by Willem Buiter. (2014). *Citi Research Economics*.
http://willembuiter.com/gold2.pdf.

[38] The seven drivers of the gold price, by Adrian Ash. (August 5th 2014). *The Telegraph*.
http://www.telegraph.co.uk/finance/personalfinance/investing/gold/11014933/The-seven-drivers-of-the-gold-price.html

[39] President Nixon ended gold convertibility in 1971. See: A Case for the World's Oldest Coin: Lydian Lion, by Reid Goldsborough. (2013).

http://rg.ancients.info/lion/article.html.

[40] World Official Gold Holdings, International Financial Statistics. (2015). *World Gold Council* http://www.gold.org/research/latest-world-official-gold-reserves

[41] Global Economic View. Gold: A Six Thousand Year-old Bubble Revisited, by Willem Buiter. (2014). *Citi Research Economics.* http://willembuiter.com/gold2.pdf.

[42] Aluminium, More Valuable than Gold!, by Window Displays. (2014). http://www.windodisplays.com/blog/aluminium-more-valuable-than-gold/.

[43] The 10 Most Important Crops in the World, by Eric Goldschein. (September 20th 2011). *Business Insider.* http://www.businessinsider.com/10-crops-that-feed-the-world-2011-9?op=1.

[44] "Guide to Commodities: Producers, Players and Prices; Markets, Consumers and Trends", by Caroline Bain. (2013). Profile Books, London, UK.

[45] "Guide to Commodities: Producers, Players and Prices; Markets, Consumers and Trends", by Caroline Bain. (2013). Profile Books, London, UK.

[46] Livestock, by Wikinvest contributors. (ND). *Wikinvest.* http://www.wikinvest.com/commodity/Livestock.

[47] The full response will not be felt immediately however, because animals in the middle of a feeding period will be fed until they reach an appropriate slaughter weight.

[48] Livestock and global change: Emerging issues for sustainable food systems, by Mario Herreroa and Philip K. Thornton. (December 2013). *Proceedings of the National Academy of*

Sciences
http://www.pnas.org/content/110/52/20878
[49] Livestock: Meat and Greens, by J. L. P. (December 31st 2013). *The Economist.* http://www.economist.com/blogs/feastandfamine/2013/12/livestock.
[50] Edible Insects: Future Prospects for Food and Feed Security, by Arnold Huis et al. (2013). *UN Food and Agricultural Organization (FAO).* http://www.fao.org/docrep/018/i3253e/i3253e.pdf.
[51] Chapter 4. Food or Fuel. In "Full Planet, Empty Plates: The New Geopolitics of Food Scarcity", by Lester R. Brown. (2012). *Earth Policy Institute.* http://www.earth-policy.org/mobile/books/fpep/fpepch4.
[52] Avoiding Bioenergy Competition for Food Crops and Land: Creating a Sustainable Food Future, Installment Nine, by Tim Searchinger and Ralph Heimlich. (2015). *World Resources Institute.* http://www.wri.org/publication/avoiding-bioenergy-competition-food-crops-and-land?utm_source=feedburner&utm_medium=feed&utm_campaign=Feed%3A+WRI_News_and_Views+%28WRI+Insights+Blog%2C+News%2C+and+Publications+%7C+World+Resources+Institute%29.
[53] Solar PV systems today can generate more than 100 times the usable energy per hectare as bioenergy.
[54] Rare Earth Elements and National Security: A CFR Energy Report, by Eugene Gholz. (October 2014). *Council on Foreign Relations Press.* http://www.cfr.org/energy-and-environment/rare-earth-elements-national-security/p33632.
[55] CRS Report Prepared for Members and

Committees of Congress: Rare Earth Elements in National Defense: Background, Oversight Issues, and Options for Congress, by Valerie Bailey Grasso. (December 23rd 2013). *Congressional Research Service.* **https://www.fas.org/sgp/crs/natsec/R41744.pdf.**
[56] Mineral Commodity Summaries. (2015). *United States Geological Survey (USGS).* **http://minerals.usgs.gov/minerals/pubs/mcs/**
[57] Why Recycle Aluminium? by Novelis Recycling UK. (ND). *Novelis Recycling UK.* **http://www.novelisrecycling.co.uk/novelis-recycling/why-recycle-aluminium/.**
[58] The World Copper Factbook. (2015). *International Copper Study Group.* **http://www.icsg.org/**
[59] Chart of the week: Oil market wobbles. (June 24th 2014). *Alpha Now* **http://alphanow.thomsonreuters.com/2014/06/chart-week-oil-market-wobbles/**
[60] Oil Prices and the Economic Recession of 2007-08, by James D. Hamilton. (June 16th 2009). *VOX.* **http://www.voxeu.org/article/did-rising-oil-prices-trigger-current-recession.**
[61] The Economic Consequences of Higher Crude Oil Prices, by Hillard G. Huntington. (2005). *US Department of Energy.* **https://web.stanford.edu/group/emf-research/docs/special_reports/EMFSR9.pdf.**
[62] By reducing the relative importance of a commodity to an economy, whether it is oil or something else, a subsequent price or supply shock may not be quite as damaging.
[63] The Economic Consequences of Higher Crude Oil Prices, by Hillard G. Huntington. (2005). *US Department of Energy.* **https://web.stanford.edu/group/emf-**

research/docs/special_reports/EMFSR9.pdf.
[64] Global Economics Paper No: 66. Building Better Global Economic BRICs, by Jim O'Neill. (2001). *Goldman Sachs*.
http://www.goldmansachs.com/our-thinking/archive/archive-pdfs/build-better-brics.pdf.
[65] Statistical Review of World Energy 2015, by BP. (2015). *BP*.
http://www.bp.com/en/global/corporate/about-bp/energy-economics/statistical-review-of-world-energy.html.
[66] Projections Show China's Grain-Hoarding Instinct, by Dim Sums. (April 30th 2014). *Dim Sums*.
http://dimsums.blogspot.co.uk/search?updated-max=2014-05-01T06:15:00-04:00&max-results=7&start=7&by-date=false.
[67] "Winner Takes All: China's Race For Resources And What It Means For Us", by Dambisa Moyo. (2012). Penguin Publishing.
[68] China's GDP is "Man-made," Unreliable: Top Leader, by Simon Rabinovitch. (December 6th 2010). *Reuters*.
http://www.reuters.com/article/2010/12/06/us-china-economy-wikileaks-idUSTRE6B527D20101206.
[69] Abusing the Li Keqiang Index?, by David Keohane. (October 28th 2014). *FT Alphaville*.
http://ftalphaville.ft.com/2014/10/28/2021252/abusing-the-li-keqiang-index/.
[70] How Chinese Commodity Financing Deals Work, And The Worry Behind Them, by Tom Vulcan. (June 5th 2014). *Hard Assets Investor*.
http://www.hardassetsinvestor.com/features/5937-how-chinese-commodity-financing-deals-work-and-the-worry-behind-them.html?showall=&fullart=1&start=3.
[71] Condemned to prosperity. (November 12th

2009). *The Economist.*
http://www.economist.com/node/14829525
[72] Dutch disease, by Wikipedia contributors.
(ND). *Wikipedia.*
https://en.wikipedia.org/wiki/Dutch_disease.
[73] Dutch disease: It's not just the oil; it's
the oil barons, by Harun Onder. (November 12th
2014). *The World Bank.*
http://blogs.worldbank.org/developmenttalk/dut
ch-disease-it-s-not-just-oil-it-s-oil-barons
[74] The Curse of Oil: The Paradox of Plenty.
(December 20th 2005). *The Economist.*
http://www.economist.com/node/5323394.
[75] "The Ascent of Money: A Financial History
of the World", by Niall Ferguson. (2008). The
Penguin Press, New York, US. pp. 26-27.
[76] Recent trends in world food commodity
prices: costs and benefits.(2011). UN Food and
Agriculture Organisation
http://www.fao.org/docrep/014/i2330e/i2330e03.
pdf
[77] Iron ore - Why the volatility in iron ore
prices? By Laura Brooks. (November 29th 2011).
CRU. http://www.crugroup.com/about-
cru/cruinsight/WhyTheVolatilityInIronOrePrices
[78] Why Food Price Volatility Doesn't Matter:
Policymakers Should Focus on Bringing Costs
Down, by Christopher B. Barrett and Marc F.
Bellemare. (July 12th 2011). *Foreign Affairs.*
http://www.foreignaffairs.com/articles/67981/c
hristopher-b-barrett-and-marc-f-bellemare/why-
food-price-volatility-doesnt-matter.
[79] Why raw materials are a dangerous
distraction, by Ricardo Hausmann. (July 29th
2014). *World Economic Forum.*
https://agenda.weforum.org/2014/07/raw-
material-value-wealth-ricardo-hausmann/
[80] UN Economic Commission for Africa:

http://www.uneca.org.
[81] Commodities for the common man, Suzanne McGee. (June 8th 2014). *The Guardian*. http://www.theguardian.com/money/us-money-blog/2014/jun/08/chocolate-orange-juice-and-gold-bars-what-commodities-mean-to-you
[82] The Real Raw Material of Wealth, by Ricardo Hausmann. (July 26th 2014). *Project Syndicate*. http://www.project-syndicate.org/commentary/ricardo-hausmann-advises-poor-countries-not-to-focus-solely-on-adding-value-to-natural-resource-exports.
[83] (America, Australia, Britain, Denmark, Finland, France, Germany, Italy, Japan, the Netherlands and Sweden.)
[84] Invisible Fuel: The Biggest Innovation in Energy is to go Without. (January 15th 2015). *The Economist*. http://www.economist.com/news/special-report/21639016-biggest-innovation-energy-go-without-invisible-fuel.
[85] Energy efficiency: The new "first fuel", by Daniel Yergin. (November 9th 2011). *Huffington Post*. http://www.huffingtonpost.com/daniel-yergin/energy-efficiency-_b_1084604.html
[86] "The Coal Question", by William Stanley Jevons. (1865). Macmillan and Co., UK.
[87] Energy efficiency gives us money to burn. (August 3rd 2013). *Tim Harford*. http://timharford.com/2013/08/energy-efficiency-gives-us-money-to-burn/
[88] The efficiency dilemma, by David Owen. (December 20th 2010). *New Yorker*. http://www.newyorker.com/magazine/2010/12/20/the-efficiency-dilemma
[89] "An Essay on the Principle of Population", by Thomas Malthus. (1798). J. Johnson, London, UK.

http://www.econlib.org/library/Malthus/malPopC over.html.

[90] For example the abolition of Britain's corn import duty, known as the Corn Laws, in 1846. See: Corn Laws, by Wikipedia contributors. (ND). *Wikipedia*.
http://en.wikipedia.org/wiki/Corn_Laws.

[91] Mad Max, by Wikipedia contributors. (ND). *Wikipedia*.
http://en.wikipedia.org/wiki/Mad_Max.

[92] "Hot Commodities: How Anyone Can Invest Profitably in the World's Best Market", by Jim Rogers. (2004). Random House Publishing Group, p. 5.

[93] Commodities and the Global Economy: Are Current High Prices the New Normal?, by Paul Bloxham, Andrew Keen and Luke Hartigan. (August 2012). *HSBC Global Research*.
https://www.research.hsbc.com/midas/Res/RDV?p= pdf&$sessionid$=GkRxhk5U2g4crjwqhtYaInw&key=U2 3WPWM8B0&n=338157.PDF.

[94] The World Copper Factbook. (2015). *International Copper Study Group*.
http://www.icsg.org/

[95] How to talk to an economist about peak oil, by James Hamilton. (July 11th 2005). *Econbrowser*.
http://econbrowser.com/archives/2005/07/how_to _talk_to

[96] Five myths about resource nationalism, by Claude Harding. (April 1st 2012). How we made it in Africa.
http://www.howwemadeitinafrica.com/five-myths- about-resource-nationalism/15042/

[97] Venezuela's Oil Diaspora: Brain Haemorrhage. (July 19th 2014). *The Economist*.
http://www.economist.com/news/americas/2160782

4-venezuelas-loss-thousands-oil-workers-has-been-other-countries-gain-brain-haemorrhage.

[98] Oil After US Hegemony, by Tyler Durden (via BofA Merrill Lynch Global Commodity Research Team). (2014). *Zero Hedge.* http://www.zerohedge.com/news/2014-08-24/oil-after-us-hegemony.

[99] Despite their name, rare earth metals (REMs) are not that rare. Many REMs are actually more abundant than some industrial and precious metals. However, it is usually hard to find a commercially viable quantity of an REE in any one location and they are difficult, expensive and environmentally-unfriendly to mine and refine.

[100] Quadrennial Defense Review . (2014). *U.S. Department of Defense.* http://archive.defense.gov/Home/features/2014/0314_sdr/qdr.aspx

[101] An Illustrated Account of the Great Maple Syrup Heist, by Lucas Adams. (January 16th 2014). *Modern Farmer.* http://modernfarmer.com/2014/01/illustrated-account-great-maple-syrup-heist/.

[102] Why does Canada have a strategic maple syrup reserve? (September 1st 2012). *Yahoo.* http://finance.yahoo.com/news/why-does-canada-strategic-maple-213000974.html

[103] Speculation and Buffer Stocks: The Legacy of Keynes and Kahn, by Luca Fantacci, Maria Cristina Marcuzzo and Annalisa Rosselli. (2012). *The European Journal of the History of Economic Thought.* 19(3): 453-473. http://www.tandfonline.com/doi/abs/10.1080/09672567.2010.501109.

[104] How Food Explains the World: From China's Strategic Pork Reserve to a Future Where Insects Are the New White Meat, 10 Reasons Why

We Really Are What We Eat, by Joshua Keating. (April 25th 2011). *Foreign Policy.* **http://foreignpolicy.com/2011/04/25/how-food-explains-the-world/.**

[105] China's Grain Stockpiling Distorts Market, by Fred Gale. (March 17th 2015). *Nikkei Asian Review.* **http://asia.nikkei.com/viewpoints/perspectives/china-s-grain-stockpiling-distorts-market**

[106] Commodity Markets Outlook, by World Bank Group. (January 2015). *A World Bank Quarterly Report.* **http://www.worldbank.org/content/dam/Worldbank/GEP/GEPcommodities/GEP2015a_commodity_Jan2015.pdf.**

[107] How Cheap Oil Has Delta Air Lines Jet Fooled, by Christopher Helman. (February 9th 2015). *Forbes.* **http://www.forbes.com/sites/christopherhelman/2015/01/21/how-cheap-oil-has-delta-air-lines-jet-fooled/.**

[108] An Airline Buys An Oil Refinery. (May 9th 2012). *The Economist.* **http://www.economist.com/blogs/gulliver/2012/05/delta-air-lines.**

[109] Shipping Rates Are Lousy For Predicting The Economy, by Vincent Fernando. (May 18th 2009). *Business Insider* **http://www.businessinsider.com/the-cost-of-global-shipping-is-a-lousy-economic-indicator-2009-5?IR=T**

[110] Cheaper Fuel to Boost Container Shipping, by John Kemp. (April 21st 2015). *Reuters.* **http://uk.reuters.com/article/2015/04/21/shipping-fuel-kemp-idUKL5N0XI3FE20150421.**

[111] Big Bottleneck: A Weak Transportation

Network Is Hurting Brazil's Once-hot Economy, by Daniel Azoulai, Henry Dunlop, and Brian Kuettel. (December 20th 2013). *Knowledge @ Wharton.*
http://knowledge.wharton.upenn.edu/article/big-bottleneck-weak-transportation-network-hurting-brazils-hot-economy/.
[112] How Many Seabirds Were Killed by the Exxon Valdez Oil Spill?, by John F. Piatt and R Glen Ford. (1996). *American Fisheries Society.*
http://alaska.usgs.gov/science/biology/seabirds_foragefish/products/publications/How_many_Sb_killed_by_Spill.pdf
[113] The Economics of Commodity Trading Firms, by Craig Pirrong. (March 2014). *Bauer College of Business, University of Houston*
http://www.bauer.uh.edu/centers/uhgemi/casedocs/The-Economics-of-Commodity-Trading-Firms-2.pdf
[114] Commodities: Tougher Times for Trading Titans, by Javier Blas. (April 14th 2013). *The Financial Times.*
http://www.ft.com/cms/s/0/250af818-a1c1-11e2-8971-00144feabdc0.html#axzz3BR0Ikpsh.
[115] Alum was an essential ingredient in textile manufacturing because it was the only substance, known at the time, to have the ability to fix natural dyes to fabrics.
[116] Those Medici. (December 23rd 1999). *The Economist.*
http://www.economist.com/node/347333.
[117] State Commodity Traders Grow to Take On Glencore, Cargill, by Javier Blas. (June 1st 2015). *Bloomberg.*
http://www.bloomberg.com/news/articles/2015-05-31/state-commodity-traders-grow-to-take-on-glencore-cargill.

[118] "High Noon for Natural Gas: The New Energy Crisis", by Julian Darley. (2004). Chelsea Green Publishing, Burlington, US.

[119] The Cure for High Commodity Prices: Human Ingenuity, by Merit Webster. (2014). *Brown Brothers Harriman Commodity Markets Update*, Issue 1. **https://www.bbh.com/wps/wcm/connect/e51f2b8043 8497ca99559f494ad2a23e/The+Cure+for+High+Commo dity+Prices.pdf?MOD=AJPERES&CACHEID=e51f2b8043 8497ca99559f494ad2a23e.**

[120] Norman Borlaug: The Genius Behind The Green Revolution, by Henry I. Miller. (January 18th 2012). *Forbes.* **http://www.forbes.com/sites/henrymiller/2012/0 1/18/norman-borlaug-the-genius-behind-the-green-revolution/.**

[121] The Real History Of Fracking, by John Manfreda. (April 13th 2015). *OilPrice.com.* **http://oilprice.com/Energy/Crude-Oil/The-Real-History-Of-Fracking.html.**

[122] Horizontal Drilling: A Technological Marvel Ignored, by David Blackmon. (January 28th 2013). *Forbes.* **http://www.forbes.com/sites/davidblackmon/2013 /01/28/horizontal-drilling-a-technological-marvel-ignored/.**

[123] Myths and Realities of Shale Gas Potential, by Mott MacDonald. (September 3rd 2013). An Energy Institute Lecture given in London, UK. **https://www.energyinst.org/filegrab/?ref=1726& f=holding-slide.pdf.**

[124] America's Shale Gas Boom Brought Rajasthan Farmers a Fortune, But Now it is Being Taken Away, John Samuel Raja. (September 1st 2014). *Quartz.* **http://qz.com/258292/how-americas-shale-gas-boom-brought-rajasthan-farmers-a-**

fortune-and-why-it-is-being-taken-away/.

[125] Fossil Fuels With $550 Billion Subsidies Hurt Renewables, by Alex Morales. (November 12th 2014). *Bloomberg*.
http://www.bloomberg.com/news/2014-11-12/fossil-fuels-with-550-billion-in-subsidy-hurt-renewables.html.

[126] The arguments against food and energy subsidies, by Jeffery Frankel. (August 18th 2014). *World Economic Forum*.
https://agenda.weforum.org/2014/08/food-energy-subsidies-egypt-india-indonesia/

[127] Nigeria faces mass strike and protests over discontinued state fuel subsidy, by Monica Mark. (January 8th 2012). *The Guardian*.
http://www.theguardian.com/world/2012/jan/08/nigeria-fuel-strike-seun-kuti

[128] "Oil 101", by Morgan Downey. (2009). Wooden Table Press LLC, New York, US. p. 322.

[129] The Effects of Climate Change on Agriculture, Land Resources, Water Resources, and Biodiversity in the United States: Synthesis and Assessment Product 4.3: Report by the U.S. Climate Change Science Program and the Subcommittee on Global Change Research, by Peter Bucklund, Anthony Janetos and David Schimel. (May 2008). *U.S. Climate Change Science Program*.
http://www.usda.gov/oce/climate_change/SAP4_3/CCSPFinalReport.pdf

[130] World Energy Outlook 2012: Executive Summary. (2012). *International Energy Agency*.
http://www.iea.org/publications/freepublications/publication/English.pdf.

[131] Fossil Industry is the Subprime Danger of this Cycle, by Ambrose Evans-Pritchard. (July 9th 2014). *The Telegraph*.

http://www.telegraph.co.uk/finance/comment/amb
roseevans_pritchard/10957292/Fossil-industry-
is-the-subprime-danger-of-this-cycle.html.
[132] White Paper: Fossil Fuel Divestment: A $5
Trillion Challenge, by Nathaniel Bullard.
(August 25th 2014). *Bloomberg New Energy
Finance*.
http://about.bnef.com/content/uploads/sites/4/
2014/08/BNEF_DOC_2014-08-25-Fossil-Fuel-
Divestment.pdf.
[133] Moving to a Low-Carbon Economy, by David
Nelson, Julia Zuckerman, Morgan Hervé-
Mignucci, Andrew Goggins and Sarah Jo
Szambelan. (October 2014). *Climate Policy
Initiative*.
http://climatepolicyinitiative.org/publication
/moving-to-a-low-carbon-economy/.
[134] Stranded Assets: What Next?, by Ashim Paun,
Zoe Knight and Wai-Shin Chan. (April 16th
2015). *HSBC Climate Change Global*.
http://www.businessgreen.com/digital_assets/87
79/hsbc_Stranded_assets_what_next.pdf.
[135] Ecological Integrity: Integrating
Environment, Conservation and Health, by David
Pimentel, Laura Westra and Reed F. Noss.
(2012). *International Journal of Epidemiology*.
31(3): 704-705.
http://ije.oxfordjournals.org/content/31/3/704
.full.
[136] How Much Water Does It Take to Make
Electricity? Natural Gas Requires the Least
Water to Produce Energy, Biofuels the Most,
According to a New Study, by Willie D. Jones.
(April 1st 2008). *IEEE Spectrum*.
http://spectrum.ieee.org/energy/environment/ho
w-much-water-does-it-take-to-make-electricity.
[137] Water Risks on the Rise for Three Global
Energy Production Hot Spots, by Tianyi Luo,

Paul Reig, Andrew Maddocks and Tara Schmidt. (November 7th 2013). *World Resources Institute*. http://www.wri.org/blog/2013/11/water-risks-rise-three-global-energy-production-hot-spots?utm_campaign=twitterfeed&utm_source=twitter.com&utm_medium=worldresources.
[138] Global Water Intelligence: http://www.globalwaterintel.com/.
[139] History, by National Water Exchange. (ND). *National Water Exchange*. https://www.waterexchange.com.au/cms/history.
[140] "Winner Takes All: China's Race For Resources And What It Means For Us", by Dambisa Moyo. (2012). Penguin Publishing.
[141] The Impact of Dodd-Frank and Conflict Minerals Reforms on Eastern Congo's Conflict, by Fidel Bafilemba, Timo Mueller and Sahsa Lezhnev. (June 2014). *The Enough Project*. http://www.enoughproject.org/files/Enough%20Project%20-%20The%20Impact%20of%20Dodd-Frank%20and%20Conflict%20Minerals%20Reforms%20on%20Eastern%20Congo%E2%80%99s%20Conflict%2010June2014.pdf.
[142] Cocoa Barometer 2015. *The Barometer Consortium* http://www.cocoabarometer.org/Barometer_2015.html.
[143] Agriculture in Ethiopia and Uganda: Not so Fair Trade. (May 19th 2014). *The Economist*. http://www.economist.com/blogs/baobab/2014/05/agriculture-ethiopia-and-uganda.
[144] Sustainability in Commodities Accrues Momentum, by Emiko Terazono. (April 20th 2015). *The Financial Times*. http://www.ft.com/cms/s/0/a935e0c8-e71d-11e4-a01c-00144feab7de.html?ftcamp=published_links%2Frss

%2Fmarkets_commodities%2Ffeed%2F%2Fproduct#axz z3Y3Jw2elm.

[145] Something to Moo Home About: Why Futures for Milk and Butter Are Making a Comeback. (April 14th 2015). *The Economist*. http://www.economist.com/news/business-and-finance/21648552-why-futures-milk-and-butter-are-making-comeback-something-moo-home-about.

[146] A single crude futures contract is for 1,000 barrels of oil, equivalent to 159,000 litres.

[147] Confusion reigns over oil prices, by John Kemp. (February 28th 2011). Financial Post. http://business.financialpost.com/investing/confusion-reigns-over-oil-prices

[148] "The King of Oil: The Secret Lives of Marc Rich", by Daniel Ammann. (2009). Macmillan.

[149] Crude Oil Price Manipulation Awakens Libor, Enron Ghosts, by Money_Morning. (May 22nd 2013). *Market Oracle*. http://www.marketoracle.co.uk/Article40558.html.

[150] The Accidental Hunt Brothers: How Institutional Investors Are Driving Up Food And Energy Prices, by Michael Masters and Adam White. (2008). http://www.loe.org/images/content/080919/Act1.pdf.

[151] Bubbles, Food Prices, and Speculation: Evidence From the CFTC's Daily Large Trader Data Files, by Nicole M. Aulerich, Scott H. Irwin and Philip Garcia. (2013). *The Economics of Food Price Volatility*. Chavas, Hummels and Wright. http://www.nber.org/papers/w19065.

[152] What Do Onion Prices Tell Us About Oil Prices? (July 9th 2008). *Time*. http://business.time.com/2008/07/09/what_do_on

ions_tell_us_about_o/

[153] How Chinese Commodity Financing Deals Work, And The Worry Behind Them, by Tom Vulcan. (June 5th 2014). *Hard Assets Investor.* http://www.hardassetsinvestor.com/features/5937-how-chinese-commodity-financing-deals-work-and-the-worry-behind-them.html?showall=&fullart=1&start=3.
[154] Squeezes, Corpses, and the Anti-Manipulation Provisions of the Commodity Exchange Act, by Craig Pirrong. (1994). *Regulation.* http://object.cato.org/sites/cato.org/files/serials/files/regulation/1994/10/v17n4-5.pdf
[155] Cocoa Cornering? The Soft Underbelly of the Commodities Markets, by Craig Pirrong. (July 20th 2010). *Seeking Alpha.* http://seekingalpha.com/article/215302-cocoa-cornering-the-soft-underbelly-of-the-commodities-markets
[156] Corners and squeezes are illegal in the US under Section 13 of the Commodity Exchange Act.
[157] California electricity crisis, by Wikipedia contributors. (ND). *Wikipedia.* https://en.m.wikipedia.org/wiki/California_electricity_crisis.
[158] Popular Delusions: Commodities for the Long Run? Not on Your Nellie – I'd Rather Eat Coal!!, by Dylan Grice. (December 15th 2010). *Societe Generale.* http://www.harringtoncooper.com/content/file/socgen%20-%20zero%20return%20on%20commodities_1382697846.pdf.
[159] Facts and Fantasies About Commodity Futures, by Gary Gorton and K. Geert

Rouwenhorst. (June 2004). *The National Bureau of Economic Research*.
http://www.nber.org/papers/w10595.
[160] How the Dumb Money Was Set Up for Commodity Failure, by Izabella Kaminska. (November 5th 2014). *FT Alphaville*.
http://ftalphaville.ft.com/2014/11/05/2030732/ how-the-dumb-money-was-set-up-for-commodity-failure/.
[161] Investors Should Abandon Long-term Commodity Bets, by a Guest Author. (December 19th 2013). *FT Alphaville*.
http://ftalphaville.ft.com/2013/12/19/1729412/ investors-should-abandon-long-term-commodity-bets/.
[162] You must check the unit size in which the bet is denominated. This can differ from firm to firm and from commodity to commodity. It is possible that a $1 a point bet could be risking $10 for every $1 movement in the commodity price.
[163] The Top Technical Indicators For Commodities Investing, by Prableen Bajpai. *Investopedia*.
http://www.investopedia.com/articles/active-trading/102314/top-technical-indicators-commodities-investing.asp
[164] Since gold is very durable, it is reasonable to assume that virtually all of the gold that has ever been refined is still out there somewhere. Gold is not consumed; it is just transformed into jewellery, while no significant depreciation of the stock occurs.
[165] Quantification of the High Level of Endogeneity and of Structural Regime Shifts in Commodity Markets, by Vladamir Filimonov, David Bicchetti, Nicolas Maystre and Didier Sornette. (2013). *Journal of International*

Money and Finance.42(C): 174-192
http://econpapers.repec.org/article/eeejimfin/
v_3a42_3ay_3a2014_3ai_3ac_3ap_3a174-192.htm
[166] Commodity Futures and Market Efficiency, by
Ladislav Kristoufek and Miloslav Vosvrda.
(2014). *Energy Economics*. 42(C): 50-57
http://econpapers.repec.org/article/eeeeneeco/
v_3a42_3ay_3a2014_3ai_3ac_3ap_3a50-57.htm
[167] Sharks Off the British Coast: Oil Tankers
Refuse to Unload Until Prices Rise... Keeping
YOUR Fuel Costs Soaring, by Ray Massey.
(November 19th 2009). *Daily Mail*.
http://www.dailymail.co.uk/news/article-
1229070/Sharks-British-coast-Oil-tankers-
refuse-unload-prices-rise--keeping-fuel-costs-
soaring.html#ixzz0XIpYdwPY.
[168] World Cup Power Cut Fears Spur Record
Brazil LNG Buying, by Isis Almeida and Lucia
Kassai. (April 25th 2014). *Bloomberg Business*.
www.bloomberg.com/news/articles/2014-04-
24/world-cup-power-cut-fears-spur-record-
brazil-lng-buying.

Printed in Great Britain
by Amazon